RIVER DAYS

EXPLORING THE CONNECTICUT RIVER FROM SOURCE TO SEA

Also Available from Appalachian Mountain Club Books

AMC River Guide: Massachusetts/Connecticut/Rhode Island, 3rd edition

AMC River Guide: New Hampshire/Vermont, 2nd edition

Massachusetts and Rhode Island Trail Guide, 7th edition

More Nature Walks in Eastern Massachusetts
　　by Michael Tougias

Nature Walks in Central and Western Massachusetts, 2nd edition
　　by Michael Tougias and René Laubach

Nature Walks in Connecticut
　　by René Laubach and Charles W. G. Smith

Nature Walks in Eastern Massachusetts, 2nd edition
　　by Michael Tougias

Nature Walks in Northern Vermont
　　by Elizabeth Bassett

Nature Walks in Southern Vermont
　　by Mark Mikolas

Quiet Water Canoe Guide: Massachusetts/Connecticut/Rhode Island
　　by Alex Wilson

Quiet Water New Hampshire and Vermont: Canoe and Kayak Guide, 2nd edition
　　by John Hayes and Alex Wilson

River Rescue: A Manual for Whitewater Safety, 3rd edition
　　by Les Bechdel and Slim Ray

Sea Kayaking along the New England Coast
　　by Tamsin Venn

*Water Trails of Western Massachusetts: AMC Paddling Guide
to the Best Lakes, Ponds, and Rivers*
　　by Charles W. G. Smith

RIVER DAYS

Exploring the Connecticut River from Source to Sea

Michael J. Tougias

Appalachian Mountain Club
Boston, Massachusetts

Cover Photograph: www.photodisc.com
All photographs by the author unless otherwise noted
Cover Design: Mac & Dent
Book Design: Stephanie Doyle
Map Design: Carol Bast Tyler

Distributed by The Globe Pequot Press, Inc., Guilford, CT

Library of Congress Cataloging-in-Publication Data is available.

The paper used in this publication meets the minimum requirements of the American National Standard for Information Sciences—Permanence of Paper for Printed Library Materials, ANSI Z39.48–1984.∞

Due to changes in conditions, use of the information in this book is at the sole risk of the user. The views presented in this book are those of the author and do not necessarily represent the views of the Appalachian Mountain Club.

Printed on recycled paper using soy-based inks.
Printed in the United States of America.

10 9 8 7 6 5 4 3 2 1   01 02 03 04 05

To my friend and fellow writer, Eric Schultz, and to my Dad, Arthur Tougias, who encouraged me to write this book.

MAP LEGEND

—————— road

⬡ interstate highway

⬭ U.S. route

⬯ state route

++++ railroad

〜 river

⤙ bridge

▰▰▰ covered bridge

XXXX dam

||| falls

Ⓛ launch (with parking)

- - - - - - portage

Ⓡ recreation area/rest stop

⛺ camping

⩑ picnic area

▲ hill/mountain

● natural area of interest

■ historic area of interest

VERMONT

NEW HAMPSHIRE

Connecticut River

MASSACHUSETTS

CONNECTICUT

CONTENTS

Acknowledgments

There are many people I'd like to thank, especially my wife, Mary Ellen, for holding down the fort while I was on the river. I would also like to thank the friends who joined me on the river: Jon Cogswell, Jim Falconer, Al Allgeier, John Griffin, Ed Hermeneau, Dave Gustafson, and Dale Queenan.

For creative suggestions that greatly enhanced the book, I'm grateful to Beth Krusi, Mark Russell, and Gordon Hardy, all fine editors and friends. I am particularly grateful to members of the Connecticut River Watershed Council who went out of their way to help me in my research, and for their efforts, and those of other groups, to clean the Connecticut.

Lastly, I'd like to acknowledge the Appalachian Mountain Club for allowing me to share my river days with readers, and AMC members whose grassroots conservation work makes outdoor recreation so much more enjoyable.

PROLOGUE

My earliest memory about the river is being awestruck. In my mind's eye I see my younger brother Mark and me, about nine and eleven years old respectively, walking through dark lowlands beneath huge maples and cottonwoods. We emerge into dazzling sunlight at the riverbank and gaze out over muddy brown water. It's an ocean, or so it seems. We have our fishing rods, but we don't cast. It's just too big—and a little bit frightening: anything could lurk in its mysterious waters.

We had good reason to feel overwhelmed by its size. Our hometown of Longmeadow, Massachusetts, abuts the widest stretch of the Connecticut River. It is 2,100 feet across there, wider than any other place on the river's journey from northern New Hampshire to Long Island Sound. Awed by the river, I found the days we spent wandering its banks some of the most satisfying of my life. We were free to follow our curiosity and impulses. The natural world was unfolding its secrets of adventure, pleasure, relaxation, and even education to us, and I've been drawn to rivers ever since.

INTRODUCTION

"We are slow to realize water, — the beauty and magic of it. It is interestingly strange to us forever..."

— Thoreau

It seems odd to me now that I would write several other books before celebrating the Connecticut River, the river of my boyhood. Maybe I was a little intimidated by its length or perhaps, as Thoreau claimed, I was slow to realize its magic. But once the paddling and hiking started there was no turning back; the river lured me onward, appealing to the what's-around-the-bend curiosity we all have.

The Connecticut laughed at my timetables. On several outings I planned just a morning trip and ended up paddling through dusk. There were just too many good places to stop and linger. The schedule for writing the book expanded from two years to four. You can't rush a river.

By the good fortune of geography the Connecticut begins in one of the most remote corners of New England. I chose to follow it downstream, traveling 410 miles southward and passing through a myriad of diverse landscapes. Starting in a boreal forest of spruce and fir, then on into lush lowlands and farming country where its west bank forms the border between Vermont and New Hampshire, the river does not encounter major cities until the Holyoke/Springfield area. The first few miles through Connecticut are developed, with Hartford and surrounding towns crowding the shore, but then the river surprises you by once again entering more natural settings. Wooded cliffs line its banks through Middletown and Haddam, and the first hints of the approaching ocean are apparent with the effect of the tides (the water appears brackish) and presence of striped bass. Numerous coves and islands enhance the last few miles before the river broadens, meeting the sea in an incredibly peaceful estuary where ospreys soar. One hundred forty-eight tributaries have now joined the Connecticut, draining 11,260 square miles to form New England's longest river.

Over the course of my travels, I came to understand how the river links past with present and humans with nature through its rich history. The Connecticut carried me past dinosaur tracks and sites of former Native American villages. It carried me through the region's first European settlements, from forts to former shipyards and even evidence of logging drives. I saw how humans altered the river with canals, ditches, dams, and reservoirs, and exploited it further through manufacturing, irrigation, and power-producing plants. But I also noted new appreciation of the river, especially recent improvements in water quality and communities working to recapture their riverfronts and establish shoreline parks and access for boaters.

I hope the reader approaches this book the same way I did my paddles, joining me on a relaxing journey to discover the river's history and natural history. *River Days* is written in a personal style, where I share my adventures, observations, elation, and even disappointments. Although not intended as a guidebook, some readers will undoubtedly want to explore sections of the river; I've included maps and a series of Explorer's Notes at the end of the book to help you plan your outing.

1

Headwaters
PITTSBURG, NEW HAMPSHIRE

Behind the customs station at the border of Pittsburg, New Hampshire, and Chartierville, Quebec, a 40-foot-wide swath has been cut through the forest to mark the international border and a faint trail follows the clearing up a steep hill. My brother Mark has agreed to join me on the first part of my exploration and we begin climbing, carefully picking our way around rocks, pausing now and then to look back over our shoulders at blue-green hills that roll into Canada. We follow the border clearing west for a half-mile then turn south onto a side trail into forest where evergreens block most of the light. In the few spots where sunlight dapples the forest floor the moss is a vivid hue of light green, almost fluorescent. The spruce and fir are healthy on these hilly peaks where the climate tends to be cool and wet. In fact, winters in Pittsburg are downright brutal with an average annual snowfall exceeding fourteen feet.

Fresh moose tracks crater the damp earth on the path. The trees are so thick a moose could be twenty yards ahead, coming toward us on the trail, and we wouldn't know until we came face-to-face. That has happened to me once before, so I peer ahead frequently. I'm also listening; maybe I'll pick up the suction sounds of hooves being pulled from the mud. Ever since a bull moose chased me, I've been wary of surprising one. Mark doesn't know it, but that's why he's leading the way down the trail.

Within minutes we are at the source of the Connecticut River, a lonely and pristine beaver pond called Fourth Connecticut Lake, resting high on the hilltop ridge, just 300 yards from the Canadian border. Surrounded by green spires of spruce and fir, and ringed by gold and green marsh grass, it's a noble beginning for the mighty Connecticut. Not all great waterways have such a pure origin. This pond and seventy-eight surrounding acres of forest were donated to The Nature Conservancy by Champion International Corporation in 1990. (Champion merged with International Paper in June of 2000.) Mark and I enjoy complete silence at this liquid jewel.

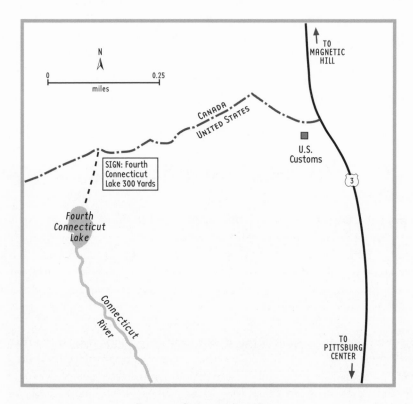

FOURTH CONNECTICUT LAKE

At the far end of the pond the branches and logs of a beaver lodge, stripped of bark and bleached by the sun, rise from the water. The pond looks to be about an acre in size and we wonder what would happen to it if the beaver move on. Would Fourth Connecticut Lake cease to exist, and if so, which of the tiny rivulets would then become the official source of the river?

The name Connecticut has its origins in the Algonquin Indian word "quinatucquet," meaning long tidal river. But as we sit by Fourth Connecticut Lake, scanning the shore for moose and beaver, it's hard to think of tides and I wonder how long it takes this water to reach the Atlantic Ocean. The drops that trickle from the pond pass along the border of Vermont and New Hampshire and through Massachusetts and Connecticut, joining with countless others to form New England's longest river.

After years of saying some day, the entire river is south of me, waiting to be explored.

❖ ❖ ❖

We retrace our steps back to the customs station and stop inside. I ask the customs officer if many people bother to make the hike up to the source.

"Oh sure," she answers. "We get all kinds. Some have gotten lost, many turn back, but the strangest of all were the two men that carried a canoe up."

Still sweating from the trail, I glance out the window behind her to see the hill we just descended.

"Did they make it?" Mark asks.

"Not sure. I know they made it to the top of the first ridge, then they were out of sight. They never stopped here to ask directions or advice about going up, and they never stopped in on their way out."

I've done some crazy things, but carrying a canoe up a half-mile ridge to launch it in an acre pond is not one of them. That's not paddling; it's portaging. Still, I admire the resolve of someone to paddle the very headwaters of the river.

The source of the Connecticut River is a lonely and pristine beaver pond called Fourth Connecticut Lake, just 300 yards from the Canadian border.

We drive south on Route 3, the same direction the river flows (still a tiny stream at this point and too small for paddling) to launch our canoe in the Third Connecticut Lake. Larger than the source, perhaps a mile long, Third Connecticut Lake is located in a valley, right next to Route 3.

There are four Connecticut lakes and each one is numbered, but to my mind the system is backward: shouldn't First Connecticut Lake be the source? Although the lake before us has no development along its shore, humans have altered it and the two lakes below. Dams built in the 1930s at the lakes' southern ends have artificially increased their area. And five-mile-long Lake Francis, which is just south of First Connecticut Lake, is completely human-made, created for flood control and storage for down-stream hydroelectric sites. Even some of the bogs are human-made, although they were created for assistance during log drives rather than flood control. Logs were held in the bogs until the high waters of spring, when they would be released and floated down the streams that feed into the Connecticut. Bogs such as East Inlet and Scott Bog were created specifically for this purpose.

We paddle on Third Connecticut Lake for a couple of hours and I use the opportunity to trail a wet fly. Brook trout or "square tails," the only trout native to New England, flourish in the cold, clean water. And, unlike the shallow pond at the source of the river, this lake has a depth of 100 feet. The trout do not cooperate but different birds entertain us: common loons, mergansers, kingfishers, and herons, we all fish the waters. Moose, which we hoped to see, are not at the lake.

Once we complete our lake paddle we drive the back roads, following the Connecticut River to Second Connecticut Lake. Both above and below Second Connecticut Lake the river surges over a boulder-strewn bed, gaining strength and flexing its muscle. Even in its beauty it has a treacherous look—certainly not the kind of water that invites canoeing. The river drops almost 200 feet between Second and First Connecticut Lake, a distance of about two and a half miles, and hard rapids continue downstream through a two-mile run from First Connecticut Lake to Lake Francis.

In the surrounding forest the spruce and fir trees seem to stretch endlessly. Most of the forest is second or third growth, having been logged for pulp and paper. Primarily owned by International Paper, the woods are crisscrossed by logging roads, many of which are open to the public. Some roads are in rough shape and four-wheel drive is essential. Others are in fairly good condition like the one leading to Scott Bog, a scenic pond located a couple miles southwest from Third Connecticut Lake.

From where we stand, evergreens appear to be the dominant trees, but Allen Petersen, a forester with International Paper, tells me northern hardwoods, consisting of such species as sugar maple, yellow birch, and beech, are actually more prevalent. The hardwoods take the best land, leaving the swampy areas and hilltops for the spruce and fir.

Since this is a managed forest, we occasionally see barren fields scarred by clearcutting. Clearcutting is considered a useful tool by foresters to regenerate stands of trees that are economically mature or of poor quality, or to create patches of young forest for wildlife habitat. Clearcutting, however, is often done for reasons that have little to do with forestry, such as converting

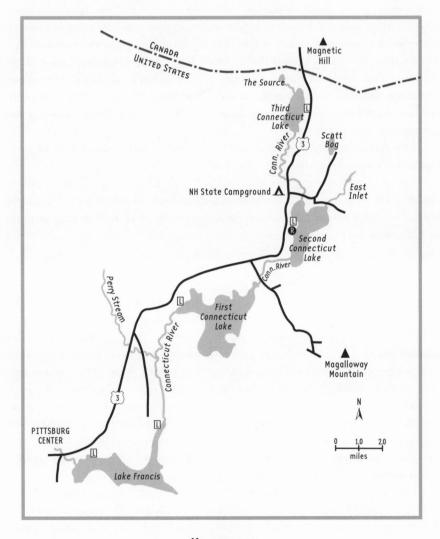

HEADWATERS

the entire value of a stand of trees to cash. Clearcutting may sometimes remove all wood from a stand of trees, including branches, stems, and leaves, a process known as whole-tree or biomass harvesting. Parts of trees not cut into logs are fed through an on-site machine that reduces them to woodchips for use as fuel or pulp. Most clearcuts regrow through natural regeneration, which in this region is rapid and abundant due to plentiful rainfall, though seedlings of desirable trees may be planted. One controversial practice involves the use of chemical herbicides, which are sprayed about five years after harvest to retard the growth of trees such as popple and pin cherry that compete with the more desirable timber of spruce and fir. As the human population grows and pressure for timber increases, our best hope is to work with paper companies rather than against them in efforts to have healthy, sustainable forests. Organizations like The Nature Conservancy have followed this approach and certain prized parcels of land have been protected through their efforts. In fact, International Paper has donated a section of undisturbed forest near East Inlet to The Nature Conservancy for permanent protection.

International Paper allows the public to use their land and logging roads and, for the most part, the public has respected paper company rules such as no camping and yielding to logging trucks. Officials at International Paper tell me that occasionally even four-wheel-drive vehicles get stuck, having confused a logging company's land with that of a state park or national forest.

❖ ❖ ❖

Mark and I drive past First Connecticut Lake, the largest of the four lakes, turn off Route 3 onto River Road, and stop at Perry Stream. While Mark sets up his easel to paint, I follow a trail downstream to the confluence of Perry Stream and the Connecticut River. I wade out into this juncture and work it thoroughly with a combination of dry flies, wet flies, and nymphs. A "brookie" finally rises to a dry fly. It's not a big fish, but oh, what colors! Red spots, a touch of gold on the belly, and a dark mottled back, which is the exact color of the river. No more trout rise, but I do not leave. The mingling of the two currents mesmerizes me. Between the powerful scent of spruce and the hypnotic effect of moving water, I find myself casting just to prolong my stay.

I think about the miles of solo paddling to come. I plan to paddle most of the river, skipping dangerous sections and several reservoirs created by dams. My goal is not to challenge the river, but to enjoy it; to get away from the work-a-day world and connect with the natural one, its peace, its rules. For people like me who are tired of this electronic age, tired of constant hype, a river trip is a therapeutic way to turn your back on it all. Pure simplicity. Elemental. Unstructured freedom. A chance to discover a less frenetic, more contemplative side of yourself. The river will show you how; it cannot be rushed, but instead sprinkles its joys in small, subtle ways.

❖ ❖ ❖

It's late afternoon when Mark and I finally leave. We drive to The Glen, a sporting lodge with cabins situated on the rocky shore of First Connecticut Lake. We plan to spend a couple of nights. Our cabin is a real classic: a cozy den with a fireplace and picture window, a small kitchen, bedroom, and bathroom. A huge meal is served family style in the lodge where we meet other guests. We trade stories and fishing hot spots and generally relax. Muscles sore from all the hiking and paddling, we rest on a large porch facing the lake, entertained by the sights and sounds of loons.

Betty Falton, owner of The Glen, joins us. She jokes that sometimes a guest arrives expecting the Holiday Inn and asking where the nearest movie theater is, when they discover there is no TV in their room. She points out that while a vacation in the North Country is not for everyone, those who appreciate rustic living and nature's beauty come back year after year.

Betty has a strong voice and is full of energy; later I'm surprised to learn she is in her 70s. Her ownership of The Glen began in 1961, but the lodge dates back to 1906. It opened as a sporting lodge called Camp Chester, then spent a period of years as a private summer place. In 1947 the Wilkinson family purchased it, reopened it as a sporting lodge, and named it The Glen. Betty and her husband, Allen, visited the region often during the 1950s, and when The Glen was for sale they bought it without hesitation. "It has been a great joy to me," explains Betty. "It's a wonderful business if you like serving people, otherwise it could be deadly! My husband passed away a few years back, but I've stayed on and hope to do so for another ten years."

She tells us a section of the cabin Mark and I are staying in was once a cabin at Metallak Lodge, located on the opposite side of First Connecticut Lake. "When it was decided in the late 1930s to raise the height of the dam on the lake," she said, "the cabin at Metallak had to be moved or it would be underwater. The folks who lived here at the time bought the cabin and used a little Yankee ingenuity to move it. They simply waited till winter, placed the cabin on logs, and used a team of horses to drag it across the ice."

"People have been visiting the region for years, escaping the city for the rugged beauty of Pittsburg. Metallak Lodge operated at the turn of the century and visitors from Boston and New York would take the train to Beecher Falls, Vermont, then stagecoach to Pittsburg Village, and finally board a special wagon to make the final leg of the trip to the lodge. It's a little easier these days."

Mark asks her about the moose. "Just wait till dusk," says Betty, "then drive along Route 3 above First Connecticut Lake; you'll see 'em." The moose apparently are attracted to the swamps near the roadside because of the salt that was spread there during winter. They start coming down from the hills and woods in May to drink the salt-laced water, and linger in the area through August. Then, as autumn approaches, they disperse back to the deep woods.

"Hunting moose in the fall," adds Betty, "is not quite as easy as it would seem because they are scattered. The real challenge, though, occurs after a moose is shot. You can imagine how tough it is to drag an animal weighing 1,000 to 1,400 pounds out of the woods."

Mark and I follow her advice. Two minutes into our drive we spot our first moose, just a few feet from the road. We stop and bolt out of the car with cameras, expecting the moose to trot off. But, as if posing for us, it merely lifts its head from feeding and stares at us with sad, large, brown eyes. Another moose comes out of the nearby spruce thicket, this one with the beginnings of antlers, about eight inches long, pointing straight out the front of its head.

Although these two moose seem tame, both bulls and cows will charge. Bulls are especially ornery from late August to October when they are in rut. If a cow is ignoring the bull during this period and you happen upon it, don't be surprised if the bull turns its frustration on you. Sometimes moose walk straight at you, allowing you time to run or climb a tree; other times they come full speed—35 miles per hour.

Driving north the few miles to the Canadian border we see a total of fifteen moose, and soon the sense of wonder we first felt starts to wane. The moose are becoming familiar, like cows in a pasture. I can understand, however, why motorists are often killed outright when a moose wanders into the road. Moose are as tall as horses. If one is standing sideways in the road a car's headlights may not fully illuminate the animal; the beams of light shine under its long legs and its eyes do not reflect light. When hit by a car a moose's body falls directly through the windshield, or its head may whip around and crash through the driver's side window. Mark and I drive slowly.

None of the fifteen moose prepares us for the final one we see in the fading light on the ride back to The Glen. It's a bull moose with a huge rack of antlers, probably over five feet across, standing next to the road looking regal and defiant. The moose we had seen earlier moved slowly, casually, but this enormous bull appears purposeful, as though it has something on its mind. It has an attitude, an attitude that demands respect. There is nothing dumb, gangly, or awkward about it. When we stop it starts off on a trot, swallowing up ground effortlessly yet still moving faster than a person could run. Cameras forgotten, we watch in awe as it passes right by us. I've got a picture imprinted on my mind forever. In fact, I'm already beginning to think twice about bushwhacking along the river for trout—what would happen if I surprised a bull moose in thick vegetation?

❖ ❖ ❖

After seeing the bull, the headwaters of the river seem wilder. Indeed this entire region has largely maintained its rugged identity, with very little encroaching development outside of the harvesting of timber. In fact, the township of Pittsburg, which covers over 300 square miles, including all the Connecticut lakes, was one of the last areas in New England to be explored by the white man.

Canadian surveyors first scouted out the hills along the headwaters of the Connecticut in 1787, and only an occasional hunting party followed them for the next ten years. Through subsequent decades a handful of settlers carved out a few homesteads and the population slowly grew. When both the United States and Canada laid claim to the region in 1832, the citizens decided to take matters into their own hands and formed an independent nation called The Indian Stream Republic.

For several years the republic made its own laws, governing (or not governing) itself accordingly. Every settler had a vote; they decided there would be no taxes, leaving town services to be performed on a voluntary basis. A 700-pound potash kettle served as the jail, and an army of forty men was formed to protect against "foreign invasion." There was little enforcement of laws and after the first few years the government fell into chaos. Citizens drifted into two camps: those that favored joining the United States and those preferring Canadian jurisdiction.

By 1835 things turned ugly. New Hampshire started sending in officers to enforce U.S. laws and a resident deputy sheriff was appointed. A Canadian sheriff, leading Indian Stream sympathizers and men from Canada, responded by kidnapping the New Hampshire deputy sheriff and hustling him north of the border. This set in motion the only skirmish. Men from U.S. river towns armed with guns, pitch forks, and scythes chased after the invaders and a fight ensued. A few men were hurt but none died, and the deputy sheriff was rescued and returned to the United States. Shortly thereafter, the disputed boundary was resolved in favor of the United States and the Republic of Indian Stream became Pittsburg, New Hampshire.

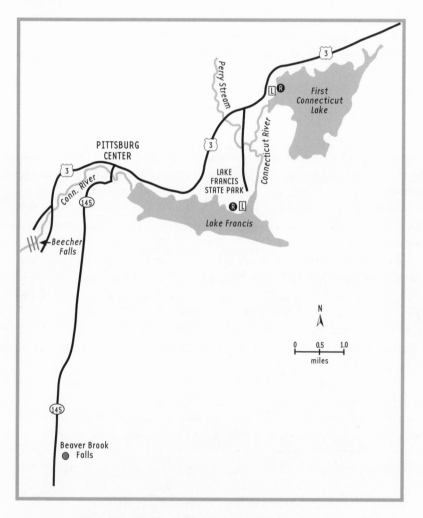

FIRST CONNECTICUT LAKE TO PITTSBURG CENTER

While the U.S. may have gotten the republic and the headwaters of the Connecticut, Canada held onto Magnetic Hill and its mysterious powers. Mark and I visit the hill, just a mile over the Canadian border in Chartierville, on the second day of our explorations. We drive to a flat area at the base of two hills where a sign in French marks the spot of the "magnetic force." Making a U-turn so the car faces the American border, we cut the engine and put it in neutral. The car starts to move slowly backward, going up the hill to our rear. We laugh like children, repeating the experiment several times. It's an optical illusion, but it certainly doesn't feel that way and I imagine a force field emanating from the nearby hills, pulling us along.

Another car with an older couple inside arrives at the site to try the experiment. The expression on the man's face as his car rolls backward up the slope is priceless, and we howl. Laughing so hard I'm near tears, I realize how good it is to act, look, and feel childlike on this lonely stretch of blacktop in Quebec, just as we did thirty years ago on the lower section of river near our boyhood home.

As a final test we stand on the road, in a perfectly flat area, and feel our bodies pulled uphill. With a little exaggeration Mark fights to stay in place, but the "force" is too strong and he is pulled backward. The man and woman in the other car stare at us, not sure if we are acting or not. They slowly drive away, the woman looking back at us several times, a concerned look on her face.

Our fun at Magnetic Hill is a good omen for the river journey. We are young boys once again.

2

PITTSBURG, NEW HAMPSHIRE, TO GUILDHALL, VERMONT/NORTHUMBERLAND, NEW HAMPSHIRE

I never seriously consider paddling the Pittsburg stretch of the river. From its source to First Connecticut Lake the river drops 800 feet, churning and swirling around countless boulders. Numerous drop-offs and almost no nearby roads make this an especially dangerous place for vessels of any kind. It's not much different between First Connecticut Lake and Lake Francis, and the thirteen-mile section running from Lake Francis to the Canaan Dam has Class II and III rapids. Adding to the difficulty are the periodic releases of water from upstream dams and a few shallow spots.

Instead, I choose to make a twelve-mile run from the West Stewartstown/Canaan bridge to the Colebrook/Lemington bridge for my first solo paddle of the year. This section of river varies from flat water to relatively easy rapids.

It's late spring and I'm staying at Timberland Lodge on First Connecticut Lake with Ed Hermeneau, one of my fishing buddies. Ed has shuttled me and my canoe to the launch site after leaving my car down-river in Colebrook. I've packed enough supplies for a small army: a cooler of food and water, camera, fishing equipment, rain gear, sunscreen, and a small electric motor. I plan on paddling the first few miles, using the motor for the last four miles where I'm told the water slows and breezes often sweep up the river, slowing your progress.

Now, as I wave goodbye to Ed, the river's current catches my canoe. I occasionally dip the paddle to stay on course, keeping the bow in the Vs that form where boulders channel the water through narrow chutes. It's a perfect day and the river sparkles in the morning sun like a thousand mirrors. Puffy cumulus clouds dot a blue sky, bird song echoes through the woods, and a sense of freedom and adventure fills me. Being alone on a river absorbs your attention; the mind empties of all other thoughts except the water and the ride. It's as if the river, the woods, and I are the only things on earth.

In a few places I float over seemingly bottomless pools that probably hold browns of legendary proportions. The New Hampshire state record brown trout was actually caught in the river in 1975 near the Pittsburg/West Stewartstown border, a gargantuan fish measuring 32.5 inches and tipping the scales at 16.5 pounds—big enough to tow my Old Town Pack canoe for quite a ride. I take a few casts from the canoe, hoping for a record of my own, and hook up with a rainbow, producing an exhilarating series of cartwheels (from the fish not me) followed by a strike from what I suspect is a nice brown that bulldogs down and rolls free.

Fighting the fish draws my attention from the river, which is why I see the fallen maple tree ahead a little late. The current wants to pull my canoe into the blowdown of branches, which acts as a strainer, letting the water go through but not me or the canoe. A shot of adrenaline courses through me. To my right is a steep bank and to the left a sandbar; I dig the paddle into the rushing water and head toward it. The canoe is now sideways and the strainer looms closer, but another pull brings me to where I can see the river bottom. Dropping the paddle and grabbing the bow rope, I hop out, slip, and get dunked, then swing the canoe to shore. Not a textbook maneuver, but it works. I vow to pay closer attention and do a better job scouting visually downstream, or there won't be many more outings. In the summer canoes will scrape and grind boulders in these rapids, but now in June after a heavy rain the river surges and flexes its muscles.

I drag the canoe over the sandbar, beyond the fallen tree and float through several narrow runs until the river widens, meandering through hayfields as if to say *what's the hurry*? But periodic rock outcroppings and ledges are still present. At one bend in the river a granite ledge gradually rises twenty feet above the water, forming a peninsula between two deep pools. The sun strikes the rock and it's simply too inviting to pass by. I swing alongside and tie up the canoe. From my earlier dip in the river I know it's freezing, but who can resist the first swim on a hot day after a long winter? I strip, stand at the edge of the ledge, and dive, hollering as soon as I surface from the numbing cold. Scrambling onto the rock I let the air warm my back before slowly easing back into the water. With goggles I swim along the base of the rock and see a trout, which looks like a small submarine, cruise away deeper into the shadows of the pool.

Feeling exhilarated, I sun myself up on the rock, and just as I'm about to drift off to sleep, I hear a voice upstream. As I wrap my towel around my waist, three kayaks zip around the bend, each with a woman paddling. They wave as they go by, moving so quickly there's no time to talk. They appear to paddle effortlessly, and I vow to buy a kayak to see if it's as much fun as it looks.

I go back to my nap, the rock radiating its heat into my cold flesh. Occasionally I look down at the dark waters of the river and, thinking I've never felt such contentment before, I declare my perch the "Rock of Contentment." No phones, faxes, or e-mail to break the mood, the Rock of Contentment allows me to appreciate the subtle therapy of moving water.

Mostly we take our rivers for granted, busy earning more money for new possessions, we forget the simple, elemental things. But even a three-hour paddle on a river a stone's throw from home can transport us to distant worlds. Seeing the world *from* a river somehow changes our viewpoint, slows racing minds, and puts us on the timetable of the natural world around us, the one we used to feel part of. When we begin to see things with a new eye, recognizing beauty in common things or reveling in the warmth of sunshine on bare skin, everyday life becomes so much richer. And once we unlock the key to really appreciating what the earth gives us, we want to experience more, to grow and connect. I think of Thoreau's *Journal* when he expressed his joy in the Concord River writing, "What an entertainment this river affords!" How he would have loved this trip down the Connecticut.

❖   ❖   ❖

Back in the canoe I paddle for three more miles, through calm water with many shallow runs over a gravel bottom. I try the fly rod and catch a small brook trout, somewhat surprised the fish I associate with mountain brooks swims in such slow water. But brook trout survive because the river's temperature stays cold, helped by the numerous streams tumbling down the mountains and into the valley. Find these little streams in the dog days of summer and there's a good chance the trout will be hanging out at their confluence with the Connecticut.

Aside from the distant murmur of a farm tractor, I sense little sign of human life. Now it's just me, a few ducks, and the river, not even any car noise droning from Route 3 on the New Hampshire side or Route 102 on the Vermont side. The locals told me I would spot moose and maybe even a bear crossing the river, but it's midday and most wildlife is probably resting until dusk. A mink, poking about the riverbank looking for frogs, birds' nests, and mice, is the only animal I see. Plenty of birds are about, however, from mergansers to great blue herons, to songbirds in the swamp maple along the shore.

I begin a twelve-mile run from the West Stewartstown/Canaan bridge to the Colebrook/ Lemington bridge, a section of flat water and easy rapids.

The final few miles before Colebrook are pretty much what I expect, placid water with little variation and many straight stretches where the wind slows my progress. I turn on my electric motor for a little extra power, and by cocking the motor all the way to one side, I'm able to paddle on the other, thereby increasing my speed to that of a kayak. The best thing about electric motors, unlike gasoline engines, is they are silent, allowing you to float down the river in peace. This little motor and my Old Town Pack canoe are probably two of the best investments I've ever made. I've had both for about ten years, and the enjoyment and adventure they afford me are chronicled in the thousands of pictures I feel compelled to take whenever canoeing. When I use the motor I feel like I'm the captain of a mighty vessel, navigating into uncharted water—even if the maximum speed is three miles an hour.

Canoes, kayaks, rowboats, even the old open-air bateaux (which look like modern drift boats) used by loggers all draft little water, allowing you into places the bigger boats can't go. Farther downriver I'll have company from motorboats, but here it's mostly paddlers and you would think the river has never experienced traffic. At the turn of the century, however, the Upper Connecticut bustled with activity during the log drives. The river would become clogged with logs and crews would stay abreast to try to keep them moving. When not in the bateau or following the log drive from shore with the aid of horses, rivermen would sometimes ride the logs themselves, paddling with a peavey or poling in shallow water with a pike pole. They often had to walk out on floating logs to pick apart a jam or plant a stick of dynamite. It was dangerous work and loggers killed in the drive were characteristically buried in pork barrels wearing their caulked boots. Even cookshacks floated down the river, mounted on huge rafts that could run the rapids. The log drives would begin just after ice-out, sometimes taking until August before the logs arrived at the mills in Massachusetts.

Signs of those days are mostly gone, but the occasional log crib, a place to hold the logs, can be seen. One such crib combined with the remains of a concrete dam lies downstream from Colebrook, New Hampshire, roughly eight miles below the Columbia covered bridge. Called Lyman Dam, this breached dam is a real hazard for boaters; large iron spikes and reinforcing steel rods lie just beneath the surface, ready to capsize or tear a hole in your vessel. I've done enough reading about the river to know Lyman Dam can be difficult to spot until it's too late. I decide to avoid it in the canoe and instead check it out by foot.

My day trip ends at the Colebrook bridge in the late afternoon. I know the river has worked its magic because when I pull ashore I realize I've been singing for the last mile.

❖   ❖   ❖

Lisa Wheeler is one of the few female fishing guides in New Hampshire, and the only female that leads both hunters and anglers. We meet at Timberland Lodge. Though my friends have had great luck fly fishing below First Lake Dam, it feels a little crowded there to me. We head instead to a stretch of riffles, rapids, and pools just below the center of Pittsburg. As we wade out into the river I ask her how she came to have such a passion for the outdoors.

"My grandfather was a guide, and I spent summers up here. He shared his skills, and over the years we explored the river and the tributaries. It was natural for me to wind up here."

I understand about natural evolution. Something or some place that excites you as a child is with you forever. My summer vacations as a boy were spent on a lake in Vermont. The whole experience became such an integral part of my growing up I bought a cabin on a pond in Vermont with the first money I saved out of college.

I ask Lisa for her perspective on guiding both males and females. She comments that "Females in general seem to be more interested in learning. Some of the fishermen I take out act like they are more interested in showing me what they know, rather than watching and listening. But mostly people just want to get away from the crowds and outwit a trout."

She then describes the river and her tactics. "The native game fish— landlocked salmon and brook trout—average about eight or nine inches, and the introduced rainbows and browns go about a foot. But there are some big brown caught in the evening."

We talk about biologists' data regarding the effect of stocked fish on native fish, and whether stocking a river can harm the native population. In rivers with heavy angling pressure and where fish are allowed to be killed, the consensus seems to be stocking makes sense. But in some waters, where catch and release is practiced, fish and game departments are experimenting with not stocking and studying how the native fish fare. (Lisa is an advocate of catch and release, using her time with clients to teach the benefits of releasing fish unharmed and helping keep the river clean.)

I tell her about the two friends staying with me at Timberland Lodge; one caught a rainbow he estimated at three pounds below First Dam, and the other landed an eighteen inch brown trout below Pittsburg on a wet fly. Lisa explains the area below First Dam usually receives a good stocking of trout, and a couple of good access routes lead from River Road to Lake Francis. Below Lake Francis, from Murphy Dam to Pittsburg, the river changes from freestone runs to gravel, with smoother gradients and probably more brown trout.

Lisa likes to fish with flies imitating the smelt and insect life of the Connecticut, and in the early spring and fall (her favorite fishing seasons) she is partial to Gray Ghosts and Magog Smelts. She matches the hatch in late spring and summer, often using Pheasant Tail Nymphs tied on size fourteen and sixteen hooks for the mayflies. For mayfly duns, she likes Sulfers and Cahills.

Before she heads back to her other job, operating Lopstick Cabins, I ask her opinion regarding my two favorite flies, the Muddler Minnow and the Woolly Bugger. "Don't know anyone who has caught much on a Muddler recently up here, but the Woolly Bugger is a great all-purpose choice."

After Lisa heads to Lopstick, I stay in the river alone, casting the Woolly Bugger to trout that will not be tempted, falling into a trance of concentration. I think of Lisa and others like her making their livings from the woods and river, and envy the lifestyle in spring, summer, and fall — but not in winter. Many people who accommodate sports enthusiasts and tourists head south in the winter, but not all, since snowmobilers also love the rugged isolation here. The owners of Timberland Lodge, Doug and Linda Feltmate, feel winter at the lodge is almost as busy as summer, explaining how the incredible amount of snow is as important to their business as the moose and trout in the summer. Doug surprised me by saying many of his guests were from New Hampshire, adding that "people who live in North Conway often come up in the summer to escape all the tourists."

As I cast, the air grows more humid, and in a few minutes a fog eases in; visibility is soon less than fifteen feet. Without seeing the river I become aware of its sounds — rushing water here, gentle ripples there — sounds so unique to rivers they cannot adequately be described by words.

Lisa Wheeler guides anglers on the river in the Pittsburg area.

❖   ❖   ❖

I have the choice of driving two roads out of Pittsburg: Route 3 hugs the Connecticut, while Route 143 runs along the crest of the river valley's eastern ridge. On the map Route 143 looks like it might have some interesting views, so I decide to follow it to Colebrook, cross the river into Vermont, and ramble along Route 102.

Just one mile into my drive along Route 145 is enough to convince me I made the right choice—the views of the valley and hillside farms are spectacular. Farther south, Beaver Brook Falls suddenly appears next to the road. I stop and walk across a field to the base of the waterfall, where erratic veins of quartz run throughout the schist ledge. The water first plunges thirty-five feet straight down before breaking into smaller cascades and pools. A fine mist carries the scent of cedar and spruce out of the woods, adding to the visual beauty.

In Colebrook I stop again, this time to look for an oddity I recall seeing many years ago. I move from store window to store window, almost giving up until I find "it" at the Mobil Station. A stuffed, two-headed calf stands in the picture window, just as it has for years. Colebrook, however, has more to recommend it. It's becoming a destination for outdoor enthusiasts and the Connecticut is one of the lures. Even moose are marketed. Driving directions to prime viewing spots are given to tourists, and in August the annual Moose Festival features a moose stew cook-off. Happily, however, Colebrook has not converted into a tourist's version of what New England should look like, nor has it succumbed to the horrors of strip malls. It's still blue collar, a real town supported by farming, standing like a frontier outpost. I like to think the people here have an inner tough-ness like the land, the kind that keeps them in a place where the average mean temperature is thirty-seven degrees. Old timers have not forgotten the past, calling the white pine "pumpkin pine" for the color of its wood, and outdoorspeople knew there were mountain lion in these hills long before it was confirmed by the biologists.

Crossing from Colebrook, New Hampshire into Vermont, I admire the lush green fields of corn growing in the rich floodplains. It is said the lowlands are free of boulders, a major benefit to the settlers that guided plows behind horse or ox. When the west opened up, farmers in much of New England left in droves for the stone-free soil of the west, but here along the Connecticut most stayed put. While farms in the hill country have reverted back to woodland, much of the land along the Connecticut is still used for agriculture. The 100-mile valley starting south of Colebrook is known as the Coos, a Abenaki term for which I have found two translations: the place of the curved river, or pine tree. No matter what the meaning, these fertile meadows are beautiful and are often referred to as the Garden of New England in recognition of the many crops grown here.

To drive Route 102 south along the river is pure pleasure, a nice view around each bend, a beckoning trout stream every mile. The fields are so lush, so green it seems like a color I've never really appreciated before. Even the pungent smell of cow manure is welcome. To me, it is not offensive, but

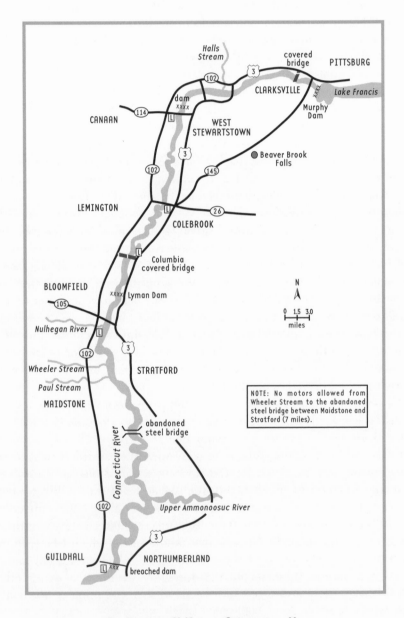

PITTSBURG, N.H., TO GUILDHALL, VT.

instead signifies true farmland, where you can almost see the cornstalks growing. (I always think of this area of New England as the North Country, but in Stewartstown a sign along the road reads "as you stand at this point on the 45th Parallel, you are halfway between the Equator and the North Pole.")

At the juncture of Lemington, Vermont, and Columbia, New Hampshire, is the Columbia covered bridge, one of those quiet places overlooked by visitors because it is set back from Route 3. Built in 1912 with Howe truss construction, it is simple yet handsome. To appreciate it fully you must walk through it, touch the old timbers, and gaze down at the river flowing below. There is something strange about being inside the dark confines of the bridge while looking out at the river, glittering in the sunlight just a few feet below.

There have been many reasons offered for why bridges were covered, most focusing on the means of travel during the 1800s and early 1900s, which was by horse. I've read that horses feared crossing water, and bridges were covered to fool the horse into thinking it was going into a barn. Another theory explains that the roof helps a horse's footing in winter by keeping out snow and ice. But the real reason was plain old Yankee frugality. The cover protects the bridge's structural timbers—the most expensive part of the bridge—from the elements, thus prolonging the life of the bridge.

At the covered bridge, I decide to make a loop of the river by driving down the Vermont side on Route 102 to the next bridge at Bloomfield, Vermont/North Stratford, New Hampshire. From there, I'll walk and fish as much of the river as possible back north to this spot.

Route 102 alternates passing through forest and farms and, in a few spots, the river flows beside the road, providing rough access. At Bloomfield, a major tributary, the Nulhegan River rolls down out of the wilds of Vermont's Northeast Kingdom. Across from the mouth of the Nulhegan in New Hampshire is North Stratford, an interesting cross-roads with a railroad yard, a stone fountain in the center of town, and what appears to be an old anti-aircraft gun aimed at the post office. I park the car and fish the stretch of river under the bridge then downstream to the Nulhegan, poking up that river before returning to the Connecticut and wading another mile downstream. By the time I return to eat my lunch by the cannon at North Stratford, I've caught three small browns.

Next, I begin to complete my loop back north to the covered bridge. A stretch of fast, rocky water catches my eye about a mile above North Stratford, where a small New Hampshire Fish and Game Department sign posted on a tree explains these waters are not stocked, containing all wild fish with special regulations in effect. Only artificial lures and flies can be used (no bait) and all fish must be released. The regulated water runs from a point 1,600 feet above the North Stratford bridge to 250 feet below the Lyman Dam. This stretch was chosen for wild trout primarily because the condition of the river, rapids with oxygenated water, is best suited for trout.

Sure enough, after bushwacking downriver, the first cast of my fly rod yields a fish that inhales the Woolly Bugger. I'm surprised to see it's a brown trout, because I usually think of browns as inhabiting slower stretches of river, and here it's all rapids with only small patches of pocket water. But browns are adaptable, if nothing else, tolerating extremely cold as well as relatively warm water, and flourishing in fast water as well as rainbows.

I follow the river upstream on foot, but the going is slow and slippery so I turn back after a mile. I'm hot, exhausted, and in a daze, not really paying attention to the alder thicket in front of me. A deep grunt just ahead stops me dead in my tracks. Something black moves and the alder trees shake. I freeze, expecting to be charged. Then nothing; no noise, no motion. I'm shaking because I know it's a bear. If it was a moose, I would have seen its head above the brush. What to do? The bear must have heard or smelled me, then jumped and growled at the same time, but it doesn't seem to have moved off. Something has to give, so I take a slow step back. No movement from the bear and I'm relieved. I retreat about twenty steps and holler so it will know I'm a human for sure. But I've still got to continue that way to get to my car. Maybe if I wait a few minutes the bear will leave, so I sit by the side of the river. I fumble around in my backpack to see if my whistle is there. It's not, but a knife is. The knife has a two and a half inch blade and looks like a pathetic weapon if the bear decides it wants me instead of the berries it was probably eating. I put the knife back in the pack; this blade would be like a pinprick to a bear. Think rationally, I tell myself; it's a black bear not a grizzly. What happened the last time I met up with a bear in the woods? It ran like hell. Then I remember before it ran, it stood up on its hind legs. Forget that thought. Time to make my move, and there's no way I'm going through that alder thicket where I can't see three feet in front of me. The river is preferable, although it's not a good wading spot. I sing to let the bear know I'm coming down the river. Half floating, half wading, I make my way to the car.

❖   ❖   ❖

Driving up Route 3, about three miles above the North Stratford bridge I see a pullout with another fishing regulation sign and a dirt road leading toward the river. I walk down and finally see the infamous Lyman Dam, and understand why it's such a hazard to paddlers. If you walk above the dam, its almost impossible to tell it's just a hundred yards down. The water is moving quickly, so paddlers may not have time to pull out on the steep banks. The drop over the remains of the cement dam is only a couple of feet, but a backwash is created that could trap a fallen paddler. In some places, iron spikes stick up from the cement and downstream is a boulder field of rapids. I'm glad I didn't canoe this stretch, especially alone, but it's well worth seeing. A large pool gathers below the dam, and I ease into the water for one last swim before heading back to the car.

Guildhall's lovely town common graced by the old Essex County Courthouse and Guildhall Community Church.

❖   ❖   ❖

One hundred forty-eight tributaries flow into the Connecticut and one of my favorites is Paul Stream in Maidstone, Vermont. Coursing down the hills of Vermont, Paul Stream is as wild a tributary as one could hope to find, with only a dirt logging road along its banks and no homes or cottages. Over the years I've fished the stream (more like a river at fifteen to twenty yards wide) and have caught brook trout in the ten inch range. Wide pools form in the river, with a couple of narrow chutes where the water thunders through mini canyons on its way to meet the Connecticut.

A few miles farther south along the Connecticut is Guildhall, with one of the loveliest town commons I've seen. The old Essex County Courthouse is next to the Guildhall Community Church, and two enormous oak trees beckon you to rest a spell, which is exactly what I do. There is something so pure, so simple about this town center. I linger for an hour, reading beneath the oaks. Occasionally I look up, wondering what it would be like to live here.

3

GUILDHALL, VERMONT, TO NEWBURY, VERMONT

We have no frying pan, butter, or salt. But we do have fresh trout in the cooler, and Jon Cogswell, a.k.a. Cogs, and I paddle the canoe to a sandy bank where we gather driftwood for a small fire. Once the fire is lit the trout are cleaned, impaled on freshly cut sticks and positioned above the flames. We lean back against an old log, stretch our legs, and turn the roasting trout. My eyes go from the magic of the dancing flames to the equally enchanting rolling river. Huck Finn never had it so good.

Our outing started at noontime in Guildhall, where we launched below the dam into a deceptively strong current. It is a fine October day, just past peak color, when the hills have taken on a rusty hue. For the first three miles we drift, never paddling, just casting. Several trout follow my lure but, when it seems they will strike, they turn aside, perhaps spooked by the sun. Finally, I hook a brown trout along a shady, boulder-strewn bank. It is a fine fish with golden flanks. Cogs gets his first strike when he roll casts a nymph under a large pine that has partially fallen into the water from an eroding bank. It, too, is a brown. We keep these first two and release the few others we catch.

At the mouth of a stream, we turn and pole our way up to a granite arch bridge where we cast to a patch of whitewater, hoping for brook trout. None obliges, but as we turn and re-enter the Connecticut, Cogs catches the biggest fish of the day—a sixteen-inch dace! I encourage him to put it in the cooler, surely it's a delicacy in some country; but he shakes his head in disgust and returns the dace to the river. Cogs, "King of the Dace," listens to my spiel on how he needs to expand his horizons, climb new mountains, tackle new challenges, and sample the taste of dace. He suggests the next fish we catch, whatever the species, must be eaten by the angler. I let the subject drop.

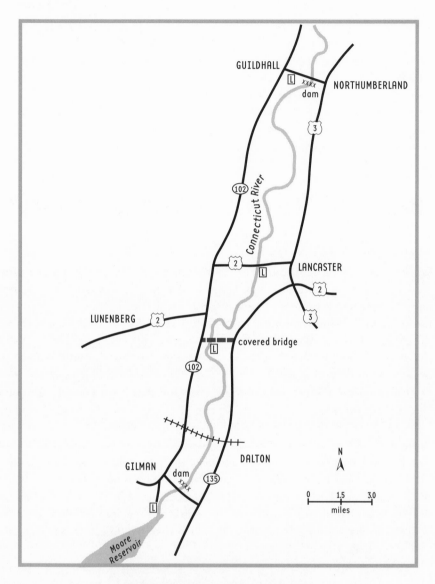

GUILDHALL, VT., TO CONCORD, VT.

Cogs and I are boyhood chums and these teasing discussions are a part of every trip. We have been traveling together for so long, even our bad trips are good trips. Our earliest explorations, going back to junior high school, were also along the Connecticut River in our hometown of Longmeadow, Massachusetts. Instead of catching trout, we wandered the floodplains along the Connecticut and angled for carp, suckers, bullhead, eels, and anything else we could find.

Two of those early forays are fresh in my mind. The first was when we explored the meadows by the river after a period of flooding and found carp trapped in a small pool that was no longer connected to the river. Occasionally, one would roll on the surface, taking our breath away as we realized they were ten- to fifteen-pounders. We cast worms and corn, but none took our offering. The water boiled with fleeing carp when our fishing weights bumped one of them. This led us to try a whole new tactic — snagging. Using giant daredevils, we raked the lure through the pond, occasionally hitting a fish. But after contact was made, our line would break, or we would reel back the lure to find only a quarter-sized carp scale impaled on the hook. For this technique to work, we needed stronger line and bigger hooks. We bicycled back to my house, returning as though we were going after swordfish or tuna: twenty pound test line and treble hooks as big as the claws of an eagle.

Admittedly, our tactics were primitive and not a practice I suggest today, but on the third cast I was fast into a big fish. It took more than one fourteen-year-old to bring it in, and Cogs had to grab my belt to keep me from slipping and sliding as I played the fish. Actually, the carp played us and soon we were covered in mud. Eventually our prize was landed, and I still have a picture of the fish and me with the mudhole in the background.

The other memory of Cogs and the river was of our hunt for lamprey eels. Each spring, these anadromous fish swam up the Connecticut from the ocean, then made their way up Longmeadow Brook. Not your foot-long, garden-variety eels, these were three-footers with bodies as thick as my forearm. Lacking jaws, as my forty-year-old encyclopedia states, "Its mouth is a round sucking organ." I couldn't have said it better myself, except perhaps to add they might be *the* most disgusting looking creatures on God's green earth. (Yet, every creature has a virtue within its own ecosystem and lampreys also can be eaten. In fact, at one time smoked lampreys were considered a delicacy in New England.)

We read how they attach their suction mouths to trout and salmon to suck their blood, and in our boyhood zeal, we used this information as an excuse to hunt them down and kill them. Our weapon of choice was a croquet mallet. On our first hunting mission, things did not go exactly as planned. As I was walking up the stream, scanning ahead for an eel to slay, I stepped on a large one that momentarily curled around my leg. Screaming, I dropped my croquet mallet in the water and ran for my life.

❖ ❖ ❖

After we cook the trout, we realize it's getting late and we still have a few miles to go to reach the car at the Route 2 bridge in Lancaster. (With only one car, I had dropped Cogs and the canoe at Guildhall, drove down to Lancaster where I left the car, then biked back up to Guildhall.) Luckily in the bottom of the canoe is our little electric motor, which we mount and cock to one side while paddling on the other. The hum of the motor competes with the distant drone of traffic, where Route 3 bends close to the river about eight miles from the start of the trip. Other signs of humankind appear, such as a series of square islands: logging cribs constructed of logs on the outside and boulders on the inside, which now sprout vegetation. Beyond the log cribs is a junkyard, with cars dating back to the 1930s and 40s spilling from the riverbank and into the water. Within these rusted hunks of twisted metal a mink prowls the shoreline, darting in and out of undercut banks and beneath car chassis. I know people in the North Country are extremely independent, resisting any restrictions on the use of their land, but I'm still surprised to find a junk-yard on the riverbank. Junkyards pose an environmental threat to the river with their leaking engine oil, gasoline, and antifreeze. It's a relief to paddle beyond the old cars and let our gaze be drawn to the Presidential Range far to the east, illuminated by the late afternoon sun in hues of pale purple.

It's after 5:00 P.M. and we have gone from paddling bare-chested to wearing flannel shirts and heavy jackets. With the sun sinking behind the mountains, the temperature has dropped about twenty degrees, and I'm beginning to wonder about my estimate of reaching the car before dark. I figured the trip would be a short one; the bike ride from where I left the car to our launching spot took me only forty minutes of fast riding. While the road was a straight line, the river snakes this way and that the farther south we go, and the current has slackened noticeably. We are both hungry and I'm beginning to wish we had roasted the dace with the trout. I mention this to Cogs, but he doesn't see the humor and asks instead if we could have paddled by the car hours ago.

By 6:30 P.M. dusk has fallen, and by 7:00 P.M. we are paddling in the dark, chilled to the bone. Not exactly the safest way to navigate a river, we have had a few near misses with boulders. As if to mock us, the river makes two large looping turns, taking us away from our southerly course. When it's too dark to write in my journal, I huddle in the bow, peering ahead for the shape of boulders. Cogs uses the treeline to steer by. Our nighttime descent into Lancaster reminds me of the many Native American raids during the French and Indian War, where braves used the river as their highway to spring attacks on downstream towns. Settlements were burned, farmers killed, and people were carried off into captivity in Canada.

I begin to tell Cogs about the Native American raids, but he isn't listening. Appearing frozen in the stern, with his hand clamped on the electric motor, face set in stony silence, Cogs is no doubt wondering how he could have been talked into another hair-brained scheme of mine.

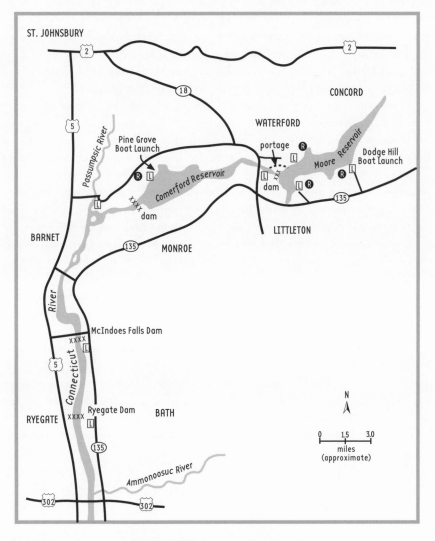

MOORE RESERVOIR TO BARNET, VT.

At 7:30 P.M., with the temperature in the low thirties, we reach the car. After blasting the heater for a few minutes, Cogs finally speaks, "That was a fine mess you got us in, Ollie."

❖   ❖   ❖

The next morning we plan to continue our paddle where Route 2 crosses the river in Lancaster, but instead get sidetracked into a little back-roading. It wasn't a conscious decision, but rather an impulsive one, caused by the excitement of seeing a large red fox on the Vermont side of the river. The fox brought back a memory of a sighting I had last summer of two young fox by the covered bridge at Lancaster. Maybe the fox before us was one of the same ones I had seen, grown from teenager to adult.

Those summer fox provided me a small adventure. When I first saw them trotting through the field by the bridge, I reached into my backpack and blew on my predator call. They stopped in their tracks, confused and curious to hear such a sound coming from a car. I got out and started taking pictures as I approached. When I was within forty feet, I could sense the fox were getting ready to run; I altered my direction so as not to head directly toward them. They let me approach within twenty feet before running into the woods. I slowly followed and was surprised to see the Connecticut River just ten feet away. I was even more surprised to see one of the fox at the river's edge, sitting and watching me. Its den, I assumed, must be very close and, sure enough, when I took another step the fox disappeared. The den was just two feet from the river beneath the roots of a spruce and a white birch. Riverfront property, not a bad spot to call home.

I take Cogs to the fox den, which is inactive, and then we head south through Dalton, a town so small it looks like the forest might swallow it up. Below Dalton the Connecticut is transformed from a river to a twelve-mile-long lake called Moore Reservoir, where osprey and bald eagles sometimes perch on dead branches. Although camping is not allowed on the reservoir, it has coves for swimming and sandy beaches for sunning. The reservoir poses two problems for canoeists: it can be quite windy and it is frequented by powerboaters. Cogs and I drive southward on a scouting mission to discover where the Connecticut becomes a river again. (If you go back in time long enough, roughly 11,000 years to the Ice Age, much of the Connecticut River was a lake, now termed Lake Hitchcock. Rubble deposited by the retreating glacier formed a great dam at Middletown, Connecticut, backing up the water northward to Norwich, Vermont. The lake was up to eight miles wide and 170 miles long until the natural dam broke, leaving the Connecticut River and a broad, fertile plain extending away from its banks.)

Just below the Moore Reservoir is the eight-mile-long Comerford Reservoir. Both reservoirs generate power when water is released through the hydroelectric stations by the dams. Although the electricity is needed, the dams and the reservoirs eliminated the best rapids on the river. Now, the river doesn't really start moving until it exits the reservoirs below the Comerford Dam. Canoe access is difficult, down a long steep hill reached from the New Hampshire side of the river off Route 135. If the station is generating at full capacity, the current can be dangerously swift, with many boulders scattered along the first two miles. Pacific Gas & Electric (PG&E) National Energy Group makes it clear this is an area for experienced canoeists only, warning "water levels often rise very rapidly as the generators come online." Paddlers are told never to camp or leave canoes unattended in the section between Comerford and McIndoes Dams. (New England Power sold all of its dams to U.S. Generating, a subsidiary of Pacific Gas & Electric, in 1998. Ownership is now under PG&E National Energy Group.)

Cogs and I scan our map and see below the Comerford Dam there are two more dams in the next twelve miles: the McIndoes Dam followed by the Ryegate Dam, known locally as Dodge Falls. The next trouble spot is the area right above Woodsville (about three miles below the Ryegate Dam), where the river makes sharp turns passing between ledges. Once again the power company issues a stern warning: "Use extreme caution during times of high water, as many canoes have capsized or taken on water at this point." With all the dams, sudden water releases, and the possibility of whirlpools forming above the mouth of the Ammonoosuc River, we continue driving south, content to skip this part of the river.

We finally find a stretch of river we both like below the confluence of the Wells River and the Ammonoosuc River. (The Abenaki names of the Connecticut tributaries roll off the tongue: the Ammonoosuc, the Ompompanoosuc, the Passumpsic.) A side road runs from Route 5 beneath a railroad trestle to the riverbank (about a quarter-mile south of Wells River Center at Route 302), leading us to a fine launch site. I drop Cogs and the canoe here, then drive south to leave the car at the boat launch by the bridge connecting Newbury and Haverhill. I estimate the paddle will cover about ten river miles.

The drive south to the take-out site is spectacular. First, a round barn sits far back in a field of grazing cows, followed by the former Placey Farm, one of the most scenic and photographed patches of real estate in

Vermont. The farmhouse and red barn lie on a hill above the river, where Route 5 makes a sweeping bend, and all are framed by the White Mountains to the east. A couple of miles south is the handsome village of Newbury, with town hall, general store, and old homes painted white encircling the common. Also on the common is the Old Methodist Church, built in 1829, which was used as a stop on the Underground Railroad for runaway slaves before the Civil War. North of the common is

The former Placey Farm in Newbury rests on a hill above the river where it makes a sweeping bend.

the Tenney Library, built in 1896, and the First Congregational Church, built in 1856, the second oldest church in Vermont. A side road leads to a tiny white home that was once the schoolhouse and is now the Oxbow Chapter of the Daughters of the American Revolution (DAR).

The whole area looks like a great place to take a walking tour, and I begin to park the car before remembering I left Cogs up the river! I never would have heard the end of it. So instead, I park the car at the bridge and bicycle back to the launch site where I find Cogs sleeping beneath a tree. Wooded islands and shallow stretches of river are the distinguishing features of the first mile of our paddle. The current is swift and in some spots navigation is difficult because of the riffles and rocky bottom. Several times the canoe becomes wedged on the rocks or grounded on the gravel bottom and we carefully pole ourselves out. (I've seen more than one canoe spill its occupants when they try to free themselves with a powerful push.)

Flocks of robins and blackbirds gather on the banks, preparing for the trip south. A lone hawk circles overhead, seemingly oblivious to the harassing crows that swoop close. At the water's edge a great blue heron stands motionless, either to conceal itself from us or perhaps from its prey in the water below. A strip of trees lines each bank and beyond the trees are cornfields. The landscape has changed since the beginning of the river; oak and maple have replaced spruce and fir, rugged mountains have given way to hills, and farms are more numerous. Here the terrain is more pastoral and gentle.

By the time we pass the Placey Farm the river is deeper and the current less noticeable—the beginning of the backwater from the Wilder Dam forty-five miles downstream. Cows come down from the fields to drink and give us blank stares as we paddle by. Boulders and rock outcroppings give the river added character as we round the bend, and the farm drops out of view.

Although we have been fishing during the entire outing, we have yet to get a strike. We've been told that walleye, northern pike, smallmouth bass, and largemouth bass occupy these waters. We later learn from another angler that our mistake is keeping our lures near the surface. His fish-finder radar shows the fish ten feet down, not far from either shore.

Once again we underestimate the length of the trip and Cogs reminds me that less is more. This time, however, we have plenty of food and eat our way south, arriving at the car with the fading light.

In our two days of canoeing we have yet to see another canoe or kayak. Maybe, it being past peak color, the tourists have scattered like the falling leaves, or perhaps few paddlers bother to venture this far north. But even here we need to protect our natural resources, or find in the future we have lost another gem from our natural world. One protection effort throughout the entire Connecticut River Watershed is the Silvio Conte National Fish and Wildlife Refuge.

The refuge will not be a typical federal park, but instead will involve the concept of a public refuge on private land, where education and enhancement of resources would be as important as the acres under the direct control of the U.S. Fish and Wildlife Service. Programs would include those that help farmers control riverbank erosion, assistance to landowners considering tax incentives in exchange for land protection and public access, and coordination for groups wishing to make the watershed more wildlife friendly. The idea is to protect and improve the river through a grassroots effort, region by region, rather than have a federally mandated program.

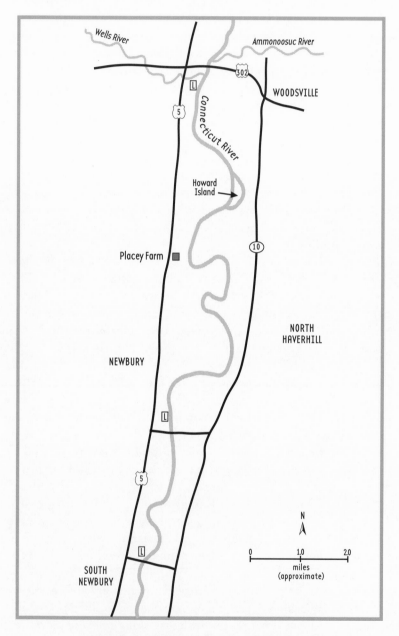

Wells River

Ammonoosuc River

302

WOODSVILLE

L

5

Connecticut River

Howard
Island →

10

Placey Farm

NORTH
HAVERHILL

NEWBURY

L

5

SOUTH
NEWBURY

L

N

0   1.0   2.0
miles
(approximate)

WOODSVILLE, N.H., TO SOUTH NEWBURY, VT.

Due to the size of the area—11,000 square miles of river basin, home to two million people in four states—collaboration might be the only way to tie all the efforts together. While the U.S. Fish and Wildlife Service may eventually buy acres deemed of critical importance, the success or failure of the concept will depend largely upon the public's involvement and the willingness of private landowners to save wildlife habitat. The concept may sound like a long shot, but consider that as recently as the 1960s and early 1970s, the river had the reputation as America's best-landscaped sewer. The Clean Water Act did wonders for the river's water quality, and maybe the Conte Refuge can do the same for wildlife habitat.

❖   ❖   ❖

Cogs and I could camp at the Haverhill Canoe Campsite on the New Hampshire side of the river, but instead we show our age and check into A Century Past Bed and Breakfast in Newbury. Innkeeper Pat Smith welcomes us and gives us a quick tour of the historic home, built in 1790, which has a cozy sitting room with fireplace. Pat tells us that after years of running the inn she thought she might retire, but the first time a realtor showed her home, she quickly took it off the market. The place was under her skin, closer to her heart than even she realized. I couldn't blame her; Newbury has its charms and her inn commands a sweeping view of the river valley. It would be a tough place to leave.

Like us, she also canoes and encourages guests to devise an itinerary where they can canoe inn-to-inn. Within the few miles of river above Lyme and Thetford there are several inns: Thetford has the Stonehouse Inn; Lyme has Alden Inn, Dowds Inn, and Breakfast on the Connecticut; Newbury has A Century Past; Ryegate has Longmeadow Inn; and Barnet has the Inn at Maplemont Farm. There is something special about being on the river all day knowing the creature comforts of a hot shower and a good meal await you at night.

The next morning during breakfast, Pat learns of my interest in history and directs us to two interesting historic markers. The first one is in the village of Wells River at the north end of Newbury. A granite sign reads, "At this point began the so called Hazen Road, running northerly fifty-four miles to Hazen's Notch in Westfield. Recommended to General Washington by General Jacob Bayley. Built by Bayley as far as Cabot in 1776. Completed by General Moses Hazen in 1779." Nearby, beneath old maples still partially cloaked in their fall splendor, is another sign pointing to the start of the trail.

Cogs and I are glad to find the sign. Over the years we have passed sections of the Bayley-Hazen Road dozens of times and even visited its terminus in the gloomy shadows of Hazen's Notch, not far from the Canadian Border. The road was an ill-conceived idea, with the intention of bringing Patriots northward to attack British strongholds in Canada. As this same road also could serve as a southerly route for the British to launch raids on the colonies, the project was abandoned.

The Wells River is the site of another obscure historical event. During the French and Indian Wars in 1759, Captain Robert Rogers led a group of colonial militia, called Rangers, on a raid against the Indians of Saint Francis in Canada. After a successful attack, the Rangers faced a challenge equal to the raid—how to return home alive. Heading south through the uncharted wilds of Vermont, they had to reach a rendezvous point on the Connecticut River before starvation and the enemy overtook them. Rogers divided his men into two groups for the purposes of finding more game and confusing the enemy. While the group Rogers led made it to the Connecticut, the French and Indians annihilated the other group.

Although Rogers' group reached the confluence of the Wells and Connecticut Rivers (a sign commemorates the day on Route 10, on the New Hampshire side of the river in North Haverhill), their hardships were not over. Assuming the Rangers would never make it, the fresh troops with supplies that were to be waiting for the group left just two hours before their arrival. Rogers wrote in his journal, "Our distress upon this occasion was truly inexpressible. Our spirits, greatly depressed by the hunger and fatigue we had already suffered, now almost sunk within us, seeing no resource left, nor any reasonable ground to hope that we should escape a most miserable death by famine." Lesser men would have given up.

The indomitable Rogers, with two Rangers and a captive Native American boy, made a desperate gamble. Making a raft of logs, they attempted to ride the Connecticut in an effort to get help at the Fort at Number Four to the south. With no dams on the river it was treacherously swift, and the foursome almost drowned in the raging currents by the falls near the White River. After five days of suffering, however, they made it to the Fort at Number four in Charlestown, New Hampshire, and sent help back for the remaining survivors.

Reading of the hardships Rogers' Rangers had getting down the river, with starvation sapping their strength, I can't help but contrast that with the peaceful day paddles we now enjoy. We think hardship is canoeing in the chill of twilight or wishing we had salt with our riverside-cooked trout.

4

NEWBURY, VERMONT, TO
HANOVER, NEW HAMPSHIRE

At 9:00 P.M. I crawl into my tent and it starts to rain. Every hour it seems to come down harder, as if someone above has a hand on the tap, opening it wider and wider. Dozing until a clap of thunder rattles me awake, I squirm to get every part of my body on the foam mattress. Years ago a friend had a close call with lighting when a strike hit the tree next to her tent, traveled into the root system she was sleeping over, and gave her a jolt while searing the bottom of the tent. Her foam sleeping pad may have saved her life.

When a particularly bright bolt illuminates the inside of my tent, I can see water pooling around the edges, the rainfly no match for a wind-driven downpour. The rain comes in buckets, the booms never cease, and sleep is out of the question. In my pack is a flashlight; I pull out my book, *A Walk in the Woods,* and read of Bill Bryson's equally uncomfortable night during a rainstorm on the Appalachian Trail. Misery does love company. I realize how lucky I am; my original plan was to canoe the river and pitch a tent on one of the river's secluded islands or sandbars. If I'd done that, I'd be in the river rather than waiting out the storm in my tent at the Pastures Campground in Orford, New Hampshire—another reminder to give the river proper respect.

In the morning light I see just how bad the storm had been. Chocolate-colored water courses down a river that normally moves at a snail's pace. Branches, trees, and flotsam float with the heavy current, giving the river a nasty, sinister look. But at least I'm safe.

Over a bacon and egg breakfast at the Fairlee Diner, the radio reports the main road to Bradford is washed out and the governor of Vermont has declared a state of emergency. The towns along the Mad River in central Vermont have been especially hard hit, with dozens of roads and homes destroyed. Two people spent the night clinging to the upper branches of a tree, as flash floods ripped their house from the foundation and swept it away. Helicopters are being used to search for more stranded people.

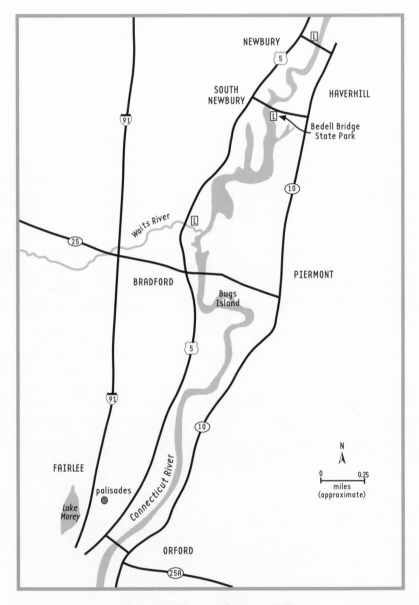

NEWBURY, VT., TO ORFORD, N.H.

I have a fifth cup of coffee—again thank my stars I didn't pitch the tent on an island—and consider my options for the day. Paddling on the river is out of the question with all the debris sailing downstream. I decide to investigate the Wilder Dam in Wilder, Vermont.

The Wilder Dam Visitor Center has a variety of displays, but it's the dam itself, or more precisely a viewing window in the fish ladder that captures my attention upon arrival. A large walleye followed by an eel swim by the window. Ten minutes later another walleye and eel struggle in the current. Not until they appear for a third time do I realize I'm seeing the same two fish. Somehow they are getting by the window only to be swept farther back before making another try.

Since the fish ladder opened in 1987, only seven salmon have made it over the dam. (Before the dams, salmon migrated all the way to Beecher Falls, Vermont.) Fish ladders certainly help the salmon going upstream, but I wonder about the hazards caused by dams to the salmon fry navigating back down the river. With or without dams, young salmon face tough odds in their survival. For every 7,500 eggs, only two will grow into adult spawning salmon. With all the difficulties mounted against salmon, I'm glad this section of river has a healthy bass population (both smallmouth and largemouth) along with walleye and northern pike. The pike in particular can grow quite large and a friend of mine once caught a four-footer in Orford. The Connecticut River may be the best-kept fishing secret in New England.

Used to generate hydroelectricity, the Wilder Dam backs up the river for a distance of forty-six miles, all the way upstream to Newbury. The dam rises fifty-nine feet from the riverbed at the site of the former Lower White River Falls (the upper falls are now under water). These were the falls in which Major Robert Rogers and his small party almost drowned. Their crude raft, hacked from white pine logs, split apart and was swept downstream, forcing Rogers to waste precious energy building another. In his memoirs he wrote, "At the bottom of these falls, while Captain Ogden and the Ranger hunted for red squirrels for a refreshment, who had the good fortune likewise to kill a partridge, I attempted the forming of a new raft.... Not being able to cut down trees, I burnt them down, and then burnt them off at proper lengths. This was our third day's work after leaving our companions. The next day we got our materials together, and completed our raft, and floated with the stream again till we came to Wattockquitchey Falls (now known as Sumner Falls), which are about fifty yards in length...." This time they were able to get to shore before the falls, but the raft was too heavy to portage. Rogers positioned himself in the freezing water below the falls to grab the raft when the Rangers let it tumble over the falls on its own. He simply writes that "I had the good fortune to succeed." Two days later they reached the Fort at Number Four in Charlestown. Ninety-two Rangers ultimately survived this mission but forty-nine died in the woods of Vermont.

❖   ❖   ❖

Not long after Rogers' harrowing raid and retreat, the French and Indian Wars ended and settlers pushed up the river, drawn by the rich soil. With depths of alluvial topsoil up to two feet and few rocks to scratch the plow, crops thrive here. The river meanders south from Newbury, traversing pastoral countryside. Signs of humans are few and far between until Bradford. The Waits River (named after one of Rogers' Rangers) enters the Connecticut on the Vermont side; about a mile below is Bugs Island. Sandy beaches are scattered about and so are signs of erosion eating into the riverbank. Some farmers blame the erosion on the dams, which frequently change the level of the water. Others blame the erosion on the wakes from powerboats, while some say it's just the work of time.

About five miles below Bradford, on the Vermont side of the river, Sawyer's Ledge overlooks the valley followed by the cliffs known as the Palisades in Fairlee. As a boy I used to climb the Palisades when my family vacationed on Lake Morey, situated less than a mile west from the river. From the summit, one has panoramic views of the Connecticut both downstream and upstream, rivaling the vista from Massachusetts' Mount Sugarloaf. Today the rocky crags of the Palisades are home to nesting peregrine falcons. To protect them, hiking is forbidden during nesting season in the spring and early summer. On a fall day, the easy half-hour climb to the summit should not be missed.

On the west side of the Palisades is Lake Morey, named for the first inventor of the steamboat, Samuel Morey. Inventing something useful, however, is different from cashing in on a new creation; Robert Fulton won that good fortune. The story behind these two men reads like a Robert Ludlum novel, with enough intrigue, twists, and turns to make the race to invent the steamboat seem reminiscent of the race to put a man on the moon.

Samuel Morey grew up along the banks of the Connecticut in Orford where his father ran the river ferry. Morey, historians say, was mechanically inclined even as a young boy, fixing neighbors' farm equipment and helping his father maintain the ferry. In 1793 he secured his first patent for a steam-powered rotisserie, but he was also at work on the steamboat, which he piloted on the river. An eyewitness wrote, "The astonishing sight of this man ascending the Connecticut River between that place and Fairlee, in a little boat just large enough to contain himself and the rude machinery connected with the steam boiler, and a handful of wood for a fire, was witnessed by the writer in his boyhood and by others who yet survive. This was as early as 1793, or earlier, and before Fulton's name had been mentioned in connection with steam navigation."

During the next three years Morey improved his design, positioning the paddle wheels to the side of a larger craft and increasing his speed to 5 MPH. His creation caught the eye of New York politician Robert Livingston, who realized the enormous potential of steam-powered navigation. Livingston offered to buy Morey's ideas and patents, but Morey refused the $7,000 proposal. It is at this point that the story becomes cloaked in intrigue and unsubstantiated stories of patent stealing. What we do know is that Livingston turned to another young engineer, Robert Fulton, and gave him the financial backing to create a steamboat that could travel up the Hudson between New York City and Albany. It's amazing what a little money can do to move an invention along. Fulton bought a Watt engine made in Great Britain and mounted two side paddle wheels on his boat, the *Clermont*, steaming from New York to Albany in thirty-two hours. He also won the patent for the side-mounted paddle wheels because Morey's earlier patent did not go into enough detail to grant exclusivity.

Morey insisted Livingston and Fulton stole his idea for the side-mounted paddle wheels; it's true Livingston not only rode on Morey's boat, but visited him at his home in Orford, looking over his engineering plans at least once. Whether or not he remembered the details of Morey's invention and passed them along to Fulton is a matter of dispute; Fulton's boat did have the same side-mounted paddle wheels as Morey's, and Fulton's successful cruise occurred fifteen years after Morey's run between Fairlee and Orford. Legend has it after Fulton received all the accolades, Morey took his boat, the *Aunt Sally*, and in a fit of anger scuttled it in the lake that bears his name.

Morey's house still stands in Orford and the town looks as if little has changed since his time. This is a compliment—the town has such a unique, handsome grace it's hard to find another in New England quite like it. The seven stately homes, known as Bulfinch Row, are what make it special. Set back behind a white fence and overlooking the town center, the homes are of the Federal style. Asher Benjamin, an associate of the famous architect Charles Bulfinch, most likely designed one of the homes, the Wheeler House, built in 1816. At the time Orford was considered a wealthy community and had about three times as many people as today.

It still appears prosperous and elegant. In the 1800s, Orford elicited even more expansive praise from Washington Irving, who wrote, "In all my travels in this country and Europe, I have never seen any village more beautiful than this. It is a charming place: nature has done her utmost here."

In Orford, seven stately homes, known as Bulfinch Row, overlook the town center.

After visiting the Wilder Dam and exploring the river by car and foot, I head back to my campsite. It looks pathetic compared to other campsites. Some have RVs with large screened tents set outside, while others have trailer tents with all the comforts of home. It wouldn't surprise me if there are faxes, answering machines, and computers in the RVs. It's beyond me why folks pack every vestige of suburbia to go camping. The more stuff you bring, the more layers between you and the outdoors.

Perhaps we have been duped by slick marketing to buy the latest and the newest even though what we have works fine. This in turn traps us in a cycle; in order to buy more, we have to work harder, all the while sapping us of our precious little free time. Equipment overload isn't limited to campers. I see anglers sweating in polypropylene waders when an old pair of sneakers works just as well in the summer. On a larger scale I see it in vacation homes. The first thing the owners do with their second home is to make it like their suburban home; planting lawns to be maintained, purchasing new furniture that cannot be sat on in a wet bathing suit, and, worst of all, posting *keep out* signs so the natives who have hunted and fished the land for generations can no longer do so.

But I'm hardly roughing it—I take a hot shower in the campground bathhouse, then settle down with another Connecticut River book titled *Voyage of the Ant*, where the author, James Dina, paddles a homemade canoe upstream from Connecticut into Massachusetts. Along the way he must forage for food and make his own shelter. Now that's roughing it.

Just as I'm about to roast a hot dog, two friends, Neal and Steve, drive up. They were supposed to arrive last night, but when they didn't show I figured they heard the weather reports predicting rain and never left Massachusetts. They had been lukewarm about the trip, preferring to stay at a motel.

I help them erect their tent. The rain starts up again so we head over to the campground's sheltered pavilion next to the river. We cook the hot dogs here, observe how the river has totally submerged the boat docks, and meet a reenactment contingent of colonial soldiers who are practicing for a Revolutionary War battle to be fought at the campground tomorrow. George Washington walks over and we invite him to join us. We learn he spends his summers getting paid to make appearances at various militia events. After discussing Washington's life and the Revolution, I ask why they are re-enacting the Battle of Fairlee if the Revolution wasn't actually fought up here. He scratches his head, then switches subjects, "What are you doing about Y2K?" he asks. In a flash we have gone from the days of muskets and powdered wigs to the day when computers supposedly will make our lives a living hell. "Have you got extra food stored away? What about backup water and heat?"

Neal comments that all he's done is make a mental note not to fly on January 1, 2000.

George shakes his head. "Son, I think you ought to be thinking about a lot more than just one day. This problem is going to affect your survival for a period of weeks."

Later, when the rain stops, we head back to the campsite, putting the predictions of gloom out of our heads while building a roaring fire. As we sit by the flames, we debate over who is going to get more firewood. This doesn't mean going into the woods with a bow saw, but rather a five-minute walk to the campground office with three dollars in hand for a bundle. Neal loses the draw and sets off on the arduous journey for firewood. He returns, not by foot, but perched on the back of the owner's truck, explaining that the bundle of wood would have been heavy to carry all the way back to the campsite. And to think we were originally going to pitch a tent somewhere alongside the river after a day of canoeing and be real outdoorsmen.

PG&E lowered the river a good four feet during the course of the night to avoid flooding, but Neal and Steve opt to paddle Lake Morey and Lake Fairlee rather than the muddy Connecticut. Even though the Connecticut is still moving a little faster than normal and the brown water looks as thick as pea soup, it seems safe enough—at least no more trees are racing down the river. I bought a kayak specifically for the river trip and I wanted to launch it in the Connecticut for its maiden voyage. Ever since seeing the kayakers glide by me upriver in West Stewartstown, I'd been saving for a kayak and now I would find out if the investment was worth it.

I launch the kayak at the campground and head downstream for a short ride, amazed at the speed I'm able to generate. It takes me all of two seconds to realize I'm going to love kayaking. A paddler sits closer to the water in a kayak than in a canoe; the double blade paddle is also a more efficient stroke. Every time you pull water back with one blade, you bring the other blade forward into position for its stroke. Not having to switch sides as in a canoe, the kayak tends to track straight. The seat has a back, allowing for greater comfort. Kayak and paddler seem to glide over the water as if on a cushion of air, and I estimate I'm going three times faster than a canoe.

For years I hesitated to buy a kayak, hearing about such maneuvers as Eskimo rolls and worrying about the claustrophobic feeling of being enclosed in a cockpit. The Old Town Loon kayak I purchased is a fire-engine red. Usually this is not my color, but its selection has something to do with turning forty. Newer model kayaks have larger and more open cockpits, and on some models it's even possible to paddle with fully bent knees—a nice change from having your legs straight in front of you. If you tip over while paddling such a model, you pop right out; your body weight simply throws you free with no special effort on your part. But don't worry about tipping over, it's nearly impossible unless you plan to paddle whitewater.

Falling into a steady pace, I paddle for ten minutes, then sip from my water bottle and rest for a bit before paddling again. I cover four and a half miles from the campground to Clay Brook in forty minutes. Continuing downstream, I slow my stroke while a light, warm rain begins to fall. My fishing rod is strapped to the side of the kayak, but with the water so muddy I'm content to enjoy the river. I pass by Lyme, New Hampshire, and Thetford, Vermont, into Norwich, Vermont, where the Ompompanoosuc River joins the Connecticut.

One of the few secluded roads along the river is found on the New Hampshire side. River Road runs parallel to the Connecticut, passing through woods, pastures, and, every now and then, offering sweeping views of the river. The rain eases and a mist settles on the river, giving me the feeling I'm paddling through an impressionist painting similar to Monet's *The Seine*. Sunlight occasionally pierces the cloud cover and it occurs to me this is the scene that elicits the expression "bathed in light." Such soft light combined with fog and mist give the river a haunting look.

After Lyme comes Hanover, New Hampshire, a popular recreational area where the river is broad and slow due to the Wilder Dam just down-stream. A year ago I paddled this stretch, first passing by the Ledyard Canoe Club and under the bridge connecting Hanover to Norwich, Vermont, then into a cove where a stream brings cold, clear water into the warm and murky Connecticut. (The cove is accessible by paddling beneath an arched granite railroad bridge. The land is owned by the award-winning Montshire Museum of Science.) Downriver about a quarter-mile is Gilman Island, which has two campsites. The island is a large one, covered with pines and hemlocks, and high enough that you don't have to worry about rising water covering your campsite. One campsite is located at the northern end, the other at the southern end, which has a picnic bench, grill, and outhouse. Some uninformed people have left trash by the fire, but otherwise the site is fine. The primitive campsite (on the northern end) is just one of many listed by the Upper River Valley Land Trust, a nonprofit organization headquartered in Hanover that is working to conserve special places in the Upper Connecticut River valley

Hanover is home to Dartmouth College where, in 1773, an energetic freshman named John Ledyard carved a dugout canoe and a place in history. At the time, Hanover was a frontier town, and Dartmouth was a college and training school for missionaries to the Native Americans. Ledyard wasn't enamored with the rigid studies, but he took full advantage of the frontier setting, taking off to spend three months with the Iroquois, apparently learning more from the natives than he did during his brief stay at Dartmouth. Upon his return to the school, he was faced with unpaid bills and tuition and decided to leave town for good—via the Connecticut River. Supplied with smoked venison and a bearskin robe, he shoved off in April, riding the river all the way home to Hartford, Connecticut. This trip was the start of a life filled with adventure; he criss-crossed the Atlantic twice in the next year and sailed with Captain Cook across the Pacific. Africa, Europe, and Asia were later destinations, and historians credit Ledyard for convincing Thomas Jefferson to sponsor Lewis and Clark's journey.

Dartmouth undergraduates commemorate Ledyard by retracing his Connecticut River sojourn, extending it to 218 miles to Long Island

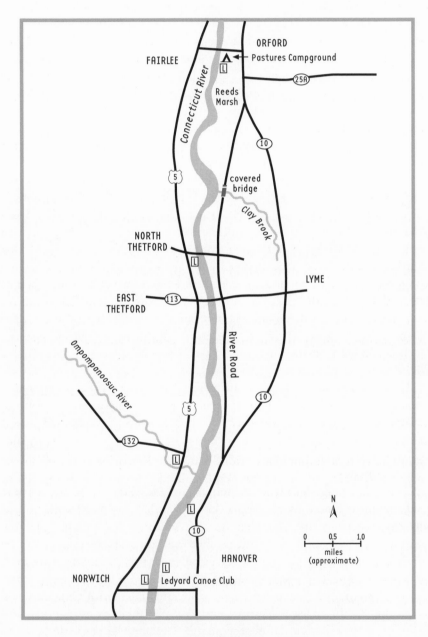

ORFORD, N.H., TO HANOVER, N.H.

Sound. Somehow these voyages evolved into races and record breaking. In 1960 two students made it to the Atlantic Ocean in an incredible thirty-three hours and fifty minutes.

❖   ❖   ❖

I'm not going to break any records today, even with a kayak. I do a U-turn as I approach Hanover, heading back upstream to Clay Brook where Neal has left my car. Clay Brook is easy to see from the river because of a covered bridge over the brook and a unique cottage at its mouth. Paddling beneath the covered bridge, I'm startled to see a moose in the water, bringing up huge mouthfuls of aquatic plants. This thing is big! I can hear it chewing; water drips from its long, homely snout. From the seat of the kayak a moose looks even more massive than it does on land. Seeing one up close and personal is a thrill. Absorbed in its eating, the moose apparently has not heard, smelled, or seen me.

I'm tempted to glide within ten feet and snap a picture of this ungainly and comical looking creature, but I learned my lesson once in Maine when I paddled too close to a bull moose. It let out a guttural grunt and made a false charge, all 1,200 pounds of it. Now I give the moose plenty of room. Finally it spots me and gives a puzzled look.

For awhile, during the mid-nineteenth century and early twentieth century, it looked as though moose would not survive, going the way of the wolf and passenger pigeon. The clearing of forestland to make pastures destroyed their habitat. Overhunting thinned their numbers to the point where the moose had disappeared from all the New England states except Maine. Moose are now back by the thousands, but I'm amazed they still prosper, especially since they seem to go out of their way to stand in front of automobiles. More than once I've driven over the crest of a hill and slammed on the brakes because a moose was in the road. Once, instead of merely trotting off to the roadside, a moose ran up the middle of the road, gangly legs pounding the pavement and head turning from side to side, making no effort to get out of the way. Finally, when it turned toward the woods it looked back at me with an odd, faraway stare, as if trying to remember what it was thinking before this shiny metal object on wheels started after it. Apparently the moose hadn't figured out that cars only stay on the roads, and perhaps was wondering if the vehicle would follow it into the woods.

One way to know if you are in moose country is to look not only for the four- to seven-inch tracks, but for more subtle signs such as browse, rubs, and rut pits. Moose eat some of the same plants deer eat, but moose browse much higher, up to seven feet off the ground. They eat aspen, willow, white birch, and mountain ash. Unlike deer, moose will also feed on balsam fir. During the fall rut, bulls will use their hooves to make rut pits or wallows, ranging from three to six inches deep. The bulls urinate in the pits, serving as a warning to other bulls that this is their territory. Tree rubs made by the moose's antlers serve a similar purpose. The way to distinguish these tree rubs from those made by a deer is again their height—a moose rub can extend up to seven feet off the ground, whereas deer rubs are usually no more than forty inches in height.

I'm startled to see a moose, bringing up huge mouthfuls of aquatic plants.

Thoreau was intrigued and puzzled by the moose's strange looks when he came face-to-face with one on a canoe trip through Maine: "Why should it stand so high at the shoulders? Why have so long a head? Why have no tail to speak of?" He thought the moose looked like "a great frightened rabbit, with their long ears and half-inquisitive, half-frightened looks: the true denizens of the forest."

The moose sighting seems like a fitting climax to an interesting excursion, so I end my paddle, load the kayak on the car, and drive to

Chapman's General Store in Fairlee for a newspaper and ice cream. When I first walk into Chapman's it looks like any other country store, until I step into the side room. Memories of the past come at me so strong they stop me in my tracks. I can almost see my father, brother, and me (at eight years old) standing and staring at the lures in the display case. Chapman's is the store that launched me into becoming a fishing fanatic. Mr. Chapman, I recall, recommended a Rapala Minnow to my Dad and told us to give it a try on Lake Morey, adding that the lake holds trophy-sized largemouth bass. After that meeting, my brother Mark and I fished almost every waking hour of our vacation, and continued to do so on Lake Morey for years.

Now here I am, thirty-six years later. Chapman's has changed very little, and it's now Mr. Chapman's son running the store, who was also just a boy when we first visited. I introduce myself and we talk about the books I've written and those I hope to write. I explain how my summers at Lake Morey had as much to do with what I've become, or haven't become, than any home I've ever lived in. If writers can trace the stirrings of the themes they chronicle, surely this was it for me.

When my family vacationed here so many years ago, we crossed the river to go to church in Orford. I would look out the car window, amazed this was the same river bordering our hometown in Massachusetts. With Ben and Jerry's New York Super Fudge Chunk in hand, I leave Fairlee and cross the river to Orford. Instead of going to church, I head down to the riverbank and celebrate middle age and the wonders of a river.

5

LEBANON, NEW HAMPSHIRE, TO SPRINGFIELD, VERMONT

When I explore one section of river, I get that what's-around-the-bend curiosity; I can't wait to move on and plan the next outing. I study topographical maps, following the curving blue strip of the Connecticut, and wonder what it will be like on the water. I consider hiking the ridges, where the contour lines on the map crowd so close together they appear as one black mass, or maybe exploring an island, backwoods pond, or some overlooked marsh. Even packing the car has an excitement, a satisfaction of getting underway for an expedition. For a weekend I am Meriwether Lewis, going into the unknown up the Missouri, or John Wesley Powell exploring the Colorado.

The drive to the river also has its moments. Thoughts are clearer when highway driving; ideas—really good ones—come popping into mind. Anticipation. The whole weekend is in front of you, the whole river waiting.

Sometimes even the radio gets me thinking. While heading up to Lebanon an advertisement along the road claims we spend 97 percent of our lives indoors. Bull, I thought. Then I did a few calculations; sleeping indoors, winter, jobs—maybe we really do spend almost every waking moment removed from God's green earth. I thought of my own situation. Up until recently that percentage was close to my own indoor-outdoor time, and it took a dark cloud to shake me out of the rat race. In the early 1990s, the company I was working for had a reengineering shuffle and the position I held was to be eliminated. That threat, along with my desire to pursue my writing and make myself more useful to family members, caused me to consider finding a position where I could work part-time.

Fear of the unknown, however, held me back and I agonized over the decision. Part-time meant less money, less security, and no more climbing the corporate ladder.

When I looked at each issue objectively, however, I found there were answers to my apprehensions. I could handle a smaller paycheck because I'd never been a slave to our consumer society. I'd easily trade more free time for fewer material possessions. The security issue gnawed at my fears of not providing for my family, but what security is there in corporate America anymore? I reasoned a diversified income, even if there was less of it, might actually make me more secure. I've always been self-sufficient, preferred prospering or suffering by my own decisions. Stepping off the corporate ladder and forgoing promotions would put me out of step with what everyone else my age was doing, but what good is a path if it doesn't follow your heart? And so, I found a part-time position and cut back on my expenses to go with the loss of income.

For me, the decision turned out to be the right one; new doors opened as soon as I shut the old one. The biggest and brightest door was the one to the outdoors, where I soon was spending about 20 percent of my time. After years of thinking about section-paddling the Connecticut, I finally had the time to do it.

I'm back on the river, driving the back roads out of Lebanon, looking for a put-in and take-out spot. I follow Route 12A southward, eyeing the river warily. According to *Canoeing on the Connecticut River* produced by PG&E, conditions change rapidly here depending on water levels, and right now the water is moving fairly quickly. Sumner Falls (also called Hartland Rapids), one of the most dangerous sections on the whole river, is just downstream. I opt not to canoe this upstream portion of river for fear of getting swept too close to the falls to turn back. Several drownings have happened at the falls, some undoubtedly canoeists who didn't know rapids were up ahead because a steep bank cuts off the view. Even wading anglers have been killed here, when water releases from the upstream dam suddenly surge through the rocky falls.

I leave the kayak on the car and bushwack down to the river with fishing rod in hand. Upstream a couple of giant boulders, known as the Chicken and Hens, jut from the water serving as a warning landmark that Sumner Falls is not far ahead. The rocks also look like a great spot for bass to rest out of the current. Just as I'm about to take my first cast, a loud *thwack* rings out, scaring the life out of me. I stumble, almost doing a belly flop into the river. At first I think someone has thrown a rock at me, but then I see the culprit looking at me from the water. Beaver. Good thing I'm not night fishing; I would have had a heart attack on the spot.

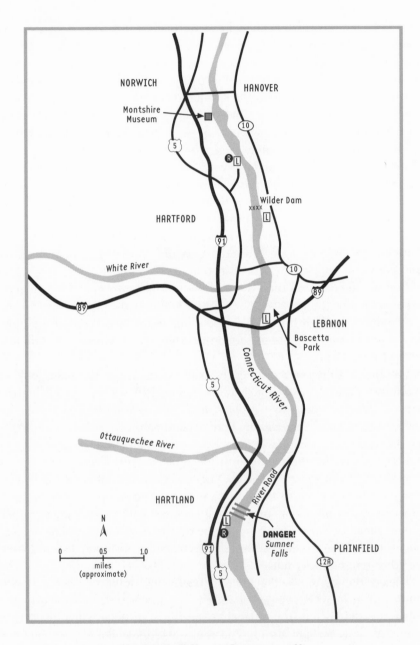

NORWICH

HANOVER

Montshire
Museum

(10)

(5)

R L

Wilder Dam

xxxx

HARTFORD

L

(91)

White River

(10)

(89)

(89)

L

LEBANON

Bascetta
Park

Connecticut River

(5)

Ottauquechee River

River Road

HARTLAND

N

0   0.5   1.0
miles
(approximate)

L
R

DANGER!
Sumner
Falls

PLAINFIELD

(91)

(12A)

(5)

HANOVER, N.H., TO PLAINFIELD, VT.

The fish are no doubt long gone. I pack up my gear, drive to the
Vermont side of the river, and start kayaking below Sumner Falls. (Access

to the falls is via a dirt road in Hartland, Vermont, near Route 5 as it crosses beneath Interstate 91.)

Flat-bottomed boats could not navigate the falls, and long ago a canal was dug on the Vermont side of the river. I consider looking for the canal, but the lure of walking out on the rocks to view the rapids is too much. In the spring the whole area is a raging torrent, but on this summer day most of the river bottom is exposed; long jagged rocks whose edges run primarily in a north-south direction. One kayaker, undoubtedly an expert, is playing in the waves and whirlpools, practicing maneuvers I'd never attempt.

One would think the bed of rock I'm standing on in the middle of the Connecticut represents the boundary between New Hampshire and Vermont, but the real boundary is on the Vermont side. After years of dispute, New Hampshire won the right to "own" the river, when the Supreme Court decided in 1933 to set the border on the west bank of the river. Old granite boundary markers, some six feet high, can still be found on the Vermont side beyond the low-water mark. Some frugal Vermonters were happy with the decision, as bridge maintenance became the duty of New Hampshire. An old yarn tells about a farmer, whose island land was thought to be in Vermont, but was really in New Hampshire. Upon learning the news he remarked, "Thank God. Didn't think I could take another one of those Vermont winters."

Nobody really owns the river, and Thoreau had it right when he wrote, "Without being the owner of any land, I find that I have a civil right to the river...I find my natural rights least infringed upon. I vastly increase my sphere and experience by boat." Of course, there is still the issue of privately owned land blocking access to the river. If a home is adjacent to the river, I always ask permission of the landowner if public access is not available. Private ownership of land can keep all of us from enjoying the water. Access to our waterways will become increasingly difficult unless we do something to protect our rights. Organizations and individuals working toward increasing public access to rivers, beaches, and lakes are vital; I lend my support to their efforts.

Can you imagine Thoreau being barred from his beloved Concord and Sudbury Rivers? He would have been like a caged bird without his daily tramps and paddles in the natural world. His journals, which delight so many of us, would have been reduced to dull political statements. Some of Thoreau's river forays are downright remarkable, particularly his up-close and personal encounter with an owl on the Sudbury River. He came around a bend in the river and saw an owl sitting on the edge of a hemlock stump. After passing the bird he got out of his boat, circled back through the woods, and caught the owl in his hands! He took the bird home, keeping it in a cage in his room before releasing it the next day. Maybe his owl-catching expedition doesn't rank up there with *Civil Disobedience*, but it's fun to read, and without access to the river, it never would have happened.

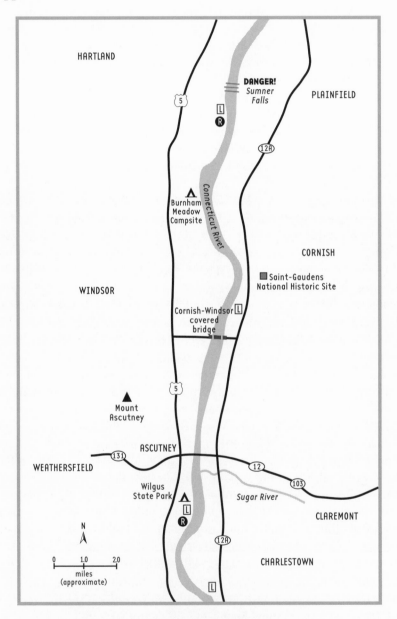

SUMNER FALLS TO ASCUTNEY/WEATHERSFIELD, VT.

❖ ❖ ❖

I launch below the falls where the river is shallow with a rock and gravel bottom—excellent trout water. My fishing rod is strapped to the kayak, but I've got my hands full navigating the current, steering around rocks as the river sweeps me through a wild forest. In a couple of spots, the kayak, which barely draws any water, grounds to a stop on the gravel bottom and the current spins me around. Only thing to do is hop out and walk the vessel down to deeper water. The effort and hassles associated with low water are well worth it; this is still one of the best paddling stretches on the entire river. The water is crystal clear; because it is shallow, often dotted with small islands, there are no powerboats. Best of all, here, the Connecticut is free-flowing—the river it was meant to be rather than a chain of reservoirs behind hydropower dams.

About a mile downriver, when the first good view of Mount Ascutney appears, fifty mergansers take flight as I round the bend. The birds are so fast that by the time I have my camera out, they're gone. Seeing mergansers on the river is a good sign. Like loons and cormorants they eat fish, diving beneath the water's surface to catch small fish in their serrated bills. Birding on the Connecticut is good through the spring, summer, and fall, and ornithologist Edward Forbush called the Connecticut River valley "the principal inland highway of bird migration within the New England states."

The mergansers must know something I don't about fishing this river. Since the trip with Cogs back up in Guildhall, I've been skunked. Even the professionals are having a hard time. A fly-fishing guide accompanied by two anglers glides by in a drift boat; they land only one trout and a couple of smallmouth bass the entire day. But from the stories I hear, the fish must be here. I meet another angler who caught a twenty-seven-inch smallmouth and a thirty-inch largemouth downstream a year ago. Sounded to me like he used the angler's "fish stretcher," but even with an exaggeration of a few inches, these would be trophy fish by any standards.

Even if the fishing were hot, I doubt I would have cast; I find a rhythm with the kayak paddle that makes me feel as though I could go all day. Somewhere around the four-mile mark I pass Hart Island and the Burnham Meadow Campsite, but I'm so into the paddling I don't recall seeing either. How could I miss fifteen-acre Hart Island? Either I'm spacing out in my old age or the river really does have the power to lull me into a trance. (At one time Hart Island was considered as a site for a hydropower dam, which would have made this incredible stretch of river another reservoir. The Connecticut River Watershed Council and other like-minded groups successfully opposed its construction.)

Another three miles of paddling brings me within sight of the Cornish-Windsor covered bridge, which, as the longest covered bridge over the river, is impossible to miss. The bridge is a photographer's dream, especially in the morning when you stand upriver and the sun illuminates both the old wooden planks and Mount Ascutney rising to the southwest. It's getting late and I beach the kayak, walk up to the bridge, and read the historic marker:

"Built in 1866, at a cost of $9,000, this is the longest wooden bridge in the United States and the longest two-span covered bridge in the world. The fourth bridge at this site, the 400-foot structure was built by Bela J. Fletcher (1811-1877) of Claremont and James F. Tasker (1826-1903) of Cornish, using a lattice truss patented by architect Ithiel Town in 1820 and 1835. Built as a toll bridge by a private corporation, the span was purchased by the state of New Hampshire in 1936 and made toll free in 1943."

The Cornish-Windsor covered bridge is a photographer's dream, especially in the morning when the sun illuminates both the old wooden planks and Mount Ascutney rising to the Southwest.

I make a mental note to return in the morning and continue paddling. I pass beneath the bridge with its massive stone pier, then beneath a railroad bridge, and finally around Chase Island, followed by a straight and slow section of river. Evening is coming on, the light is soft, and nobody else is on the river. Crickets hum along the shore and the scent of water, fresh and clean, adds to my sense of well-being. You can't beat dawn and dusk on a river.

Another hour of paddling and I finally reach North Star Canoe Rentals in Cornish, where I've arranged a lift back to my car. From the start of my outing at Sumner Falls to my take-out point at North Star Canoe Rentals, I've covered about twelve miles in four and a half hours of steady paddling. Most people take twice that long in canoes, enjoying frequent stops to picnic, swim, or fish.

I chat with the folks at North Star, but I'm not much company; totally bushed from the paddling, I struggle to keep my eyes open. Outside, the covered bridge's wooden windows glow yellow from the inside lights. A soft intermittent rain is falling, and a bit of fog hangs over the black river. Maybe a good rain will pick up the current for tomorrow's paddle. Thoreau wrote in his *Journal*, "Let it rain heavily one whole day, and the river will be increased from a half dozen rods in width to nearly a mile in some places, and where I walked a dry-shod yesterday a-maying, I sail with a smacking breeze today, and I fancy that I am a sailor on the ocean."

I recall the flood the night I was camping back in Orford and I'm glad tonight I won't have to worry about the elements; I'm staying at the Chase House Bed and Breakfast in Cornish, New Hampshire, a mile from the bridge. The inn is actually two houses blended into one: a 1775 Federal-style house and a 1766 Colonial. Salmon Chase was born in the house in 1808. He went on to hold a wide variety of political positions, including senator, secretary of the treasury under Lincoln, founder of the Republican party, and chief justice of the Supreme Court.

After sleeping like a zombie at the Chase House, I awake early and take a bike ride north along the river before breakfast. Cycling, like canoeing and kayaking, allows me to notice the little things like the wild flowers, ferns, and berries that line the road. A layer of fog floats above the river, obscuring the lowlands but not the top of Mount Ascutney, which rises into clear blue sky. The best visual treat of all is north of the covered bridge at the Saint-Gaudens National Historic Site. The property was the home of Augustus Saint-Gaudens, a sculptor who created works of bronze and marble. Re-creations of his work are on display in the gardens, including the monument to Civil War leader Colonel Shaw leading black troops into battle.

It is early morning and none of the buildings are open, but I'm free to wander the incredible gardens. Besides the formal flower gardens a long path runs through a tunnel of birch trees illuminated by the morning sun. I'm convinced recognizing the beauty around us is the first step to a higher consciousness—and a happier life.

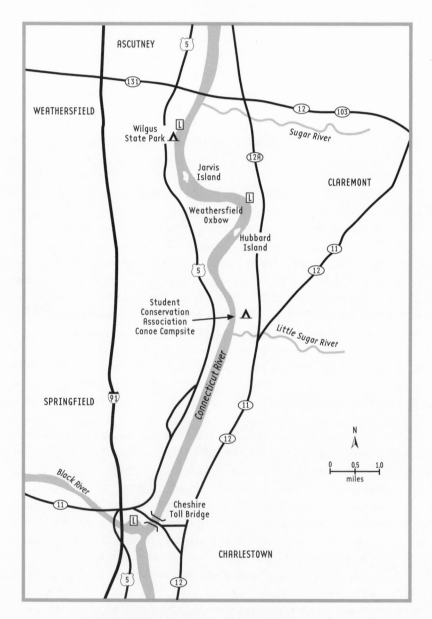

ASCUTNEY/WEATHERSFIELD, VT., TO SPRINGFIELD, VT.

One of the real problems with solo paddling is how to get back to your car when the trip is over. Fortunately for those who like to bicycle, peddle power can be combined with paddle power to provide a solution. On this morning, I first leave my kayak at Wilgus State Park in Weathersfield, Vermont, drive downstream into Springfield, Vermont, park my car, and bike back up to my kayak. I think of the trip as a way to get exercise, and this works both the legs and arms. As an added bonus I'm seeing the river from two different perspectives.

I plan to paddle about ten miles, but when I launch the kayak, I realize it will be a rough outing. Temperatures are in the nineties and a strong wind is coming at me from the south, kicking up waves that spray over the bow. Had I been in a canoe, I would have a hellish time being buffeted about by the gusts. The kayak, which is more aerodynamic and rides low to the water, cuts through the wind a bit more effectively. Still, after the first hour of paddling, my triceps have a burning feeling from being overworked, and I pull to a shaded cove and take a swim. The cool water rejuvenates me and for the rest of the trip I set a moderate pace, pausing every fifteen minutes to rest and drink from my water bottle.

I break up the monotony of hard paddling by shifting position, some-times putting my legs outside the cockpit and along the top of the kayak. Other times I focus solely on the rhythm of the strokes, even closing my eyes for short periods. It's amazing how as soon as you stop relying on sight you become more conscious of your other senses—I smell that wonderful water scent and hear every sound within a quarter-mile, or so it seems. A month earlier I led a group of visually impaired people on a nature walk, and through them learned to enhance my other senses. I found I could identify trees by touch and smell. The smooth bark of birch and beech were easy to distinguish, and with practice, even the maple, ash, and oak. For evergreens, I used my nose, detecting a subtle difference between crushed pine needles and hemlock.

Now, with eyes closed, the lapping waves and the warmth of sun on bare skin lull me. But the reverie doesn't last long—in the distance is the drone of approaching motors. Unlike yesterday's paddle, where the river was swift and shallow, this section is slow and deep, and you've got to share the water with boats more suited to the ocean than a river. As the day goes on, more motorboats charge past, sometimes staring at my kayak and me as if I am from Mars. In a twelve-foot kayak with big boats motoring by, I feel like I am from another planet, or maybe another century. I just hope all this traffic, myself included, is not having an adverse effect on the river.

Since the Clean Water Act of 1972, we have done a remarkably good job ferreting out direct discharges from industry and sewer pipes.

These sources involve well-defined releases, which can be measured and monitored at the point of entry to the river. The next battleground is the nonpoint source pollution, which is caused by rainfall and melting snow seeping into the ground. As this runoff seeps, it carries away pollutants, including bacteria from failed septic systems, sediment from poorly managed construction sites, and fertilizers from farms, all of which are diffuse in nature making them more difficult to identify and control. Even less obvious are other pollutants, such as oil and gas runoff from streets, and chlorine used to disinfect water prior to drinking. Treating lawns and gardens with pesticides, herbicides, and chemical fertilizers also adds to the problem. As nonpoint source pollution finds its way into the river or leaches into the groundwater, it can be harmful to fish and other aquatic life and to our drinking water.

❖　❖　❖

Not all the boats are zooming by. A few motor past at cruising speed and wave to me, as if out for a Sunday drive on a back road. Some even stop to talk, and I meet a husband and wife in a small duck-hunting boat who are poking around a cove. They tell me they have been exploring the Connecticut together for over thirty years. I comment on how the trees along the river are all scarred fifteen feet up and ask if it's from the ice in the spring. "Yes," says the woman. "You should have seen it here in March of 1977. Ice floes crashed into the bridge by our house with such force, I thought it would surely collapse." Now the man warms to the story: "Those same ice floes, combined with flooding, eroded the riverbank below our house and we had to have huge boulders trucked in as riprap to save the hill."

Continuing downstream, I first pass Jarvis Island, then a launch site on the New Hampshire side, followed by Hubbard Island and the confluence of the Little Sugar River. A number of homes, mostly on the ridgeline above the Vermont side, look down on the river. When I was looking for a place to leave my car downstream, I didn't realize there was a major boat launch in Springfield by the Cheshire Toll Bridge. I got permission from a home-owner with a dock on the river. I see his dock, pull over, and he helps me carry the kayak up to the car. A friend is visiting and she laughs and runs over to shake my hand. "You won't believe this," she says with a big smile, "but I saw the flash of your red kayak going down the river while I was driving way up on Route 5 near Ascutney. It looked like such fun and I sud-denly wanted a kayak of my own. Then you disappeared from view, and now, three hours later, here you are pulling out at the very house where I'm visiting."

6

CHARLESTOWN, NEW HAMPSHIRE, TO BELLOWS FALLS, VERMONT

One of my favorite places on the river, and one of the least known, is the Fort at Number Four, an exact re-creation of a colonial fort in Charlestown, New Hampshire. To walk through the fort, particularly if you are the first one inside in the morning, is about as close as you can get to stepping back into the eighteenth century when the French and Native Americans were at war with the colonies.

From the seat of my canoe, I see the fort's log palisade rising above the river on a little knoll, much the same way the Native Americans would have seen it while advancing on a raid. I beach the canoe, walk up to the stockade, and have the sensation that I've been here before. It's a quiet Sunday morning and I stroll through the main gate, feeling as lucky as a kid on Christmas morning.

The unusual name of the fort originates from the land-grant plantations chartered here by the Massachusetts Bay Colony; the fourth such land grant was here at Charlestown. It must have taken more than a little courage for settlers to venture to this northernmost outpost on the river in 1740, when Native American hostilities were so great. Ever since the end of King Philip's Indian War—when most of the Native Americans of southern New England were killed, sold into slavery, or fled north to Canada—war parties of Native Americans used the Connecticut River valley to launch raids on English settlements to the south. Despite this threat, ten families had settled at the Fort at Number Four by 1744. Once their dwellings were erected, they began construction of the fort, knowing, if attacked, they were on their own—the nearest settlement was thirty miles away.

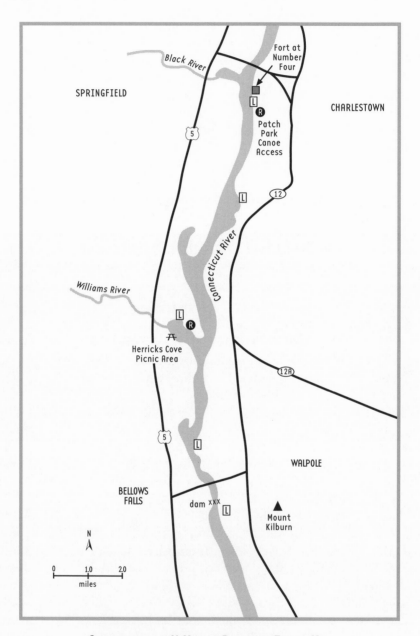

Fort at Number Four

Black River

SPRINGFIELD

CHARLESTOWN

5

L
R
Patch Park Canoe Access

L

12

Connecticut River

Williams River

L
R

Herricks Cove Picnic Area

12A

5

L

WALPOLE

BELLOWS FALLS

dam xxx   L

Mount Kilburn

N

0   1.0   2.0
miles

CHARLESTOWN, N.H., TO BELLOWS FALLS, VT.

The settlers showed sound judgement in choosing their captain, Phineas Stevens. As a boy, Native Americans had taken him captive to Canada. His knowledge of the Native Americans from living among them gave him insight few other white men had of their habits and rituals.

The fort was erected none too soon, as the first foray by Native Americans occurred in 1745: two settlers were killed while working in the fields outside the fort and another was taken captive. This was to be the start of years of continuous raids. Often times the Native Americans would lie concealed outside the fort's log stockade, swooping upon settlers who ventured out to tend to the livestock or crops. After two years of devastating hit-and-run attacks, the weary settlers abandoned the fort just before the winter of 1746–47.

The next spring Captain Stevens and thirty men marched back to the fort, expecting it to be in ashes. Instead they found the fort exactly as they left it; even a dog and cat that had been abandoned were still alive. Just days after Stevens' arrival on April 7, 1747, a party of some 500 Native Americans and their French commanders attacked the fort. Stevens describes the scene as follows: "The wind being very high and every thing exceeding dry, they set fires to all ye old fences, they also set fire to a Log house about 40 rods distance from ye fort to ye windward, so in a few minutes we were entirely surrounded with Fire. All which was performed with ye most hideous shouting and firing from all quarters, which they continued in a very terrible manner until ye next day at 10 at night, without Intermission, in which term of time, we had no opportunity either to Eat or Sleep..."

For three days the siege went on, and the enemy continued to try to burn the fort by shooting flaming arrows and rolling burning carts to the stockade walls. But the fort was well built for defense, and the thirty men inside were able to hold off the enemy with musket fire. Finally, the French commander called an end to the attack. Of the thirty men serving under Captain Stevens, none was killed and only one was wounded.

Settlement at the fort resumed, but so did sporadic Native American raids. In 1754 several settlers were taken captive, including Mrs. Susanna Johnson who meticulously chronicled her travail upon her eventual release. She writes that prior to her capture the summer of 1753 was peaceful and that "The inhabitants in NO. 4, and its vicinity, relaxed their watchfulness, and ventured more boldly into the fields. Mr. Johnson now thought himself justified in removing to his farm, an hundred rods distant from the fort, which was then the uppermost settlement on the Connecticut River..."

Mr. Johnson was a little premature in thinking the area safe. On August 29, 1754, the family was attacked. The Johnsons, along with their neighbors, were captured and forced to march to Canada. Their story is like so many other unlucky victims of the war, except Mrs. Johnson not only had to endure being captured by Native Americans, she was also pregnant. On the second day of captivity she delivered a healthy baby girl,

One of my favorite places on the river is the Fort at Number Four, an exact re-creation of a colonial fort in Charlestown, N.H.

whom she named Captive. Both mother and baby survived the ordeal and eventually were freed after long months in Canada.

When I poke my head inside the dark homes within the fort, it's impossible not to think of Mrs. Johnson and all the other unfortunate settlers. Why did they risk life and limb to carve out a home in this dangerous wilderness, knowing they were the northernmost settlement? Was it for land? The prospect of wealth? Or did they wish to distance themselves from the long arm of Puritan rigidity that extended from Boston? Certainly one thing is for sure, these people were made of a stuff far tougher than we can even imagine.

Inside the fort I meet historical interpreter Miles Keefe, and mention the courage of these people. "They really were tough as nails—it's not a cliché," says Miles. "Think about the obstacles they faced: wolves, Indians, smallpox, and more." As we walk through the homes, which range from little more than a lean-to with dirt floors to larger buildings with plaster walls, Miles refers to the fort as the "Alamo of the East." "The French and Indian Wars went on for so long our society was completely militarized for years upon years," he says.

From a lofty perch in the lookout tower, I get a bird's-eye view of the fort below and the slow-moving waters of the Connecticut. I notice that the logs in the stockade are set a few inches apart with nothing between them. Couldn't the enemy rush the walls and shoot through the openings?

Miles explains there were two reasons for this construction. Without the openings snow could drift up against the walls, making it easier for the enemy to climb over. The spacing also was used to prevent the spread of fire: if a flaming arrow hit one log, it would be difficult for the flames to jump to adjacent logs.

The exact site of the original fort is actually a short distance away on a higher patch of ground, now marked by a boulder on Route 12. Before the fort, the settlers built a few simple homes at the center of town, and then built the fort's stockade around the heart of the town. Those unlucky souls whose homes were outside of the town's center often had to move back and forth between their farms and the fort, tending their fields during the daytime and sleeping in the fort at night. Staying at their homes was a tremendous risk the Johnsons and other farmers took with varying degrees of success.

I walk from building to building, inspecting the doctor's chambers, the fur-trapping implements, and the blacksmith's shop, all the while wondering if there is such a thing as reincarnation. Everything looks so familiar. Two authentic dugout canoes catch my eye; both were found in the muck at the bottom of New Hampshire lakes. Next to these is a birch-bark canoe made by an Abenaki in Quebec. The handsome vessel is aged to a golden hue and about the same size and shape as my Old Town Pack canoe, except without the seat. Seeing the canoes brings me out of my history trance; it's time to head back to the river.

Earlier, I put in at the public launch at the mouth of the Black River in Springfield, Vermont, just below the Cheshire Toll Bridge (the last of the Connecticut River's thirty-three toll bridges). Now, after visiting the fort, I have to get on with the business of getting downstream. It isn't going to be easy—again the wind is coming up the river from the south. Whitecaps, mini-rollers, rogue waves: the water sounds like the ocean and I feel like I'm battling *The Perfect Storm*.

To make matters worse, numerous motorboats are on the river, accessing the water at launches by the Cheshire Bridge in Charlestown, New Hampshire, and downstream at Herricks Cove. The bass boats, especially, seem a bit ridiculous; racing at full speed, then coming to a quick stop where the anglers cast furiously. One fisherman in the bow, another in the stern, each takes about ten casts—maybe changing lures once—then off they zoom to the next likely spot. Two anglers who stop nearby look grim, as if smallmouth-bass fishing is a job. Must be a tournament, I reason, but still, whatever happened to sitting, fishing, and maybe talking a little?

The bank on the New Hampshire side of the river, about twenty feet high, is eroding, and every now and then I hear the plop of dirt falling into the river. Even the experts aren't sure whether this is natural or a result of powerboat wakes. I try to hug the shore and stay out of the way of the boats, but the shallows are like a minefield of stumps, many submerged just below the surface.

This is the first day on the river I do not enjoy. I've had both slow and boring days of paddling, but never an outing where I'm more tense on the river than in my car. I'm paddling not for pleasure, but merely to reach the take-out at Herricks Cove. I think of a canoeist who wrote a book about paddling the Hudson. Sometimes while reading it, I could sense he was having a bad day and just wanted to get the trip over with. I'm determined that after today this won't happen to me again. Flexibility will be my guide, and I won't schedule any taxing paddles. It's best to linger where it suits you, skipping or rushing through the areas that don't, or else you sacrifice the fun of the journey for the destination, defeating the purpose

A great blue heron slowly stalks the riverbank, hunting for snakes, frogs, fish, and even small birds.

of your coming in the first place. Author William Least Heat Moon said it best when he warned: "Too rigid an itinerary ruins the trip." I'll take his advice and just go with the flow.

I still have a couple of miles to go before reaching my bike at Herricks Cove, so I paddle out of the main river and into backwater, eating my lunch as the breeze pushes the canoe along. When the canoe floats to the back end of the cove, a few minutes pass before I realize I have company. A great blue heron is standing twenty feet away. I stop chewing and sit motionless, trying to match the stillness of the bird. For a few minutes we just watch each other. Then slowly it pushes off, spreads its wings, and is airborne, surprisingly graceful for a bird its size. With long legs trailing, the heron silently curls to the south and vanishes over the treetops. This, I think, is why I come back to the river; these little moments of beauty make me feel part of the natural world.

I'm seeing more great blue herons on New England's rivers than ever before. Their populations are rising because reduced water pollution equates to more fish, and herons are voracious eaters. They slowly stalk a riverbank, then in a lightning-fast move snatch a fish or even a frog, snake, or small bird. I once saw one grab a small sunfish and flip it so it went down its throat headfirst. Getting a snake down isn't so easy. On a different outing I watched a heron take fifteen minutes to swallow a snake!

Another reason for the heron's come back is the increase in the beaver population. More beaver mean more beaver ponds, which are the preferred nesting sites of great blue heron. The heron make their nests of sticks atop the standing dead timber in the beaver ponds; apparently the water thwarts raiding raccoons, the main predator of their fledglings and eggs.

Seeing the heron (or maybe it was eating my lunch) has a calming effect and I resume paddling. Unfortunately, the worst of my day is yet to come. I begin to cross the river, hoping the Vermont side will provide better cover from the wind, and I notice a boat coming upriver at full speed. As it approaches, the driver actually alters his course so the boat points directly at me. All I can do is be ready to dive overboard. At the last possible minute the boat veers off. The driver, a young man with blond hair, is laughing as the huge wake from his boat overtakes my canoe. Quickly, trying to control my seething rage, I point the bow of my canoe directly into the oncoming wave and avoid capsizing.

After the powerboat incident, I sit rocking on the waves. I think about what another paddler, Rob Perkins, said about powerboats in this very same stretch of river. Perkins canoed the length of the Connecticut and chronicled his trip in a quirky yet highly entertaining documentary. He mounted a camcorder to the front of his birch-bark canoe and left it running, catching the spontaneity of the trip and all his comments, including his ruminations on powerboats, which he calls stinkpots. He opens a segment of the video by saying, "What a beautiful morning it is; how quiet, how peaceful." Then the audience hears the oncoming drone of an engine and Perkins captures a boat speeding by. He sadly remarks, "They don't even slow for birch bark. How can they appreciate nature roaring and whizzing past it...."

Another part of Perkins' film captures his marvelous wit and has always stayed with me. Perkins comes upon a bear hunter who has just killed a bear. While the hunter describes the excitement of the sport, Perkins, who is troubled by the killing, muses live on camera, "I don't know if Mr. Bear wanted to be part of your sport."

Now I feel like Mr. Bear; I didn't really want to be part of the motorboat's sport, but there's little I can do to improve boating etiquette.

7

BELLOWS FALLS, VERMONT, TO THE MASSACHUSETTS BORDER

If you are going to make a long paddle in the vicinity of Bellows Falls, try to have a car waiting above the dam and falls to avoid portaging by foot. The term *portage* is stretching it—you have to carry your canoe a half-mile through town to get back onto the river.

Bellows Falls has a distinctive look and feel. A travel writer described Bellows Falls as having the flavor of an Italian hill town, which it does, particularly with Mount Kilburn looming on the other side of the river. The industrial past is certainly evident in the old buildings lining the curving street, which are mixed pleasantly with residential areas. Through the gaps in the buildings you can see the green hills of the countryside.

On the negative side, the town would be all the more interesting if the great falls on the Connecticut had not been altered by the hydroelectric dam. Except in the springtime when the dam is opened, the narrow gorge is dry, looking more like a canyon out west than a riverbed. Imagine how incredible this town would be if the thundering falls and gorge were still in their natural state rather than harnessed for power. Imagine, too, that not long ago twenty-five-pound salmon congregated here, gathering strength before leaping the churning levels of the falls. (The salmon were so numerous that in colonial times apprentices had clauses in their contracts, limiting the number of salmon meals they could be served in a week.) Of course, the Native Americans were also here, and from a spot near the Vilas Bridge you can see petroglyphs on the rocks by the river. The carvings of human faces are said to be the work of Abenakis and could date from several thousand years ago to just four hundred years ago.

A number of the round faces have horns or prolonged projections, but no one seems to know exactly why.

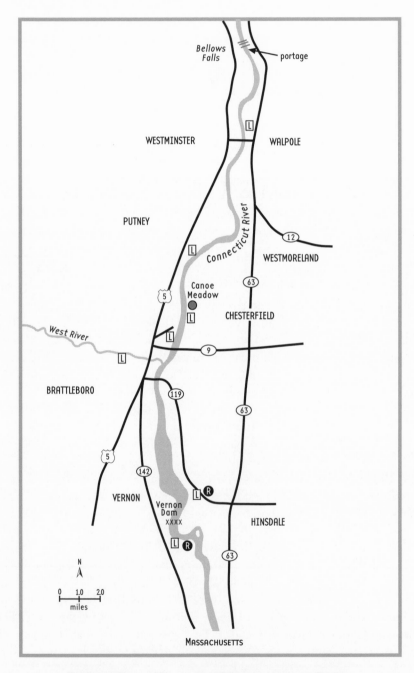

BELLOWS FALLS, VT., TO THE MASSACHUSETTS BORDER

We may not know the purpose the Native Americans had for the carvings, but another resident, Hetty Green, had intentions that were quite clear: make money and hold onto it. Green, known as the witch of Wall Street, lived on the corner of School and Westminster Streets. She successfully played the market in good times and bad (actually predicting the crash of 1907), and at the time of her death in 1916 was regarded as the richest woman in the world. She spent little on comforts, and her hoarding may have actually cost her son his leg. Apparently, Green took so long to find cheap medical attention for him his leg had to be amputated.

Long before Hetty Green came to Bellows Falls, one of America's first canals was built here so boats could continue upstream and logs could come down. Completed in 1802, the original canal required nine locks and ten years of construction to bypass the fifty-foot falls. The most famous of the steamboats to come through the canal was the *Barnet*; built in 1826 with the single-minded purpose of navigating the river from Connecticut to Barnet, Vermont. The owners wanted to prove the proposed Farmington Canal (from New Haven, Connecticut, to Northampton, Massachusetts) was not needed. The goal was to show that upstream navigation was possible simply by powering through the Enfield Rapids and bypassing the falls at Bellows Falls via the canal. The *Barnet* struggled at the Enfield Rapids, and it took a scow lashed to either side and thirty men with poles to conquer the rapids. After getting through the rapids it seemed the boat would be home free. But there was one little problem at Bellows Falls: the *Barnet* was too wide to make it through the canal. Imagine building a boat for the single purpose of making it to Barnet, Vermont, and forgetting to measure the width of the Bellows Falls canal first. The *Barnet* had to turn stern and steam back south, although its owners tried to salvage the trip by saying it proved upstream navigation possible. Shortly thereafter, another steamer, the *William Hall*, made it to the same spot and was also too wide for the narrow canal. Rather than turn back, however, the captain hired a team of oxen and had the boat towed through the streets to a spot above the falls, where it then continued on to Hartland.

Despite these setbacks, canal fever gripped New England, and plans were actually drawn to connect the Connecticut River with Lake Champlain. In the flowery prose of yesterday, a newspaper reporter wrote that "We most earnestly hope that the fever will not abate until the cooling waters of the Connecticut shall meet and mingle with those of Lake Champlain."

❖ ❖ ❖

After encountering too many powerboats on my last outing, I decide today's trip will be a short one in case the river has weekend crowds. I find a landing in Putney, by the Putney Inn off Route 5, and launch my canoe, heading downstream. At a small island, over a hundred butterflies are dipping in the water and I try to capture it on film. The butterflies seem a good omen for the day, and the river looks beautiful: broad with large cottonwood trees lining the banks and forested hills rising beyond. But with each passing mile more powerboats appear and I realize I should have gone upstream where the river is shallower. Soon, I meet a kayaker who has come from Bellows Falls, and he tells me the ten-mile stretch below the dam had some quick water and no whizzing powerboats. It's too late to turn back; my bicycle is chained to a tree downriver in Brattleboro.

I make the best of the trip, stopping often to loll in the shade and finish a book I can't seem to put down about an incredible river journey. *Undaunted Courage*, by Stephen Ambrose, chronicles the Lewis and Clark expedition in such an entertaining and informative way, it sweeps you up in the adventure and makes you want to read late into the night.

The number one supporter of the expedition was President Thomas Jefferson, who anxiously wanted to establish an American presence in the Pacific Northwest and wrestle the fur trade away from the British. In fact, before the Lewis and Clark expedition was launched, John Ledyard, the same Ledyard who canoed down the Connecticut from Dartmouth, proposed his own exploration of the North American continent to Jefferson. Ledyard's plan was to travel to Moscow, cross Siberia, and hitch a ride on a Russian fur-trade vessel across the Bering Sea. He would then cross the North American continent on foot. Instead of a large contingent of fellow explorers, he proposed to do this with his two dogs! As far-fetched as it sounds, Jefferson was supportive, showing just how badly he wanted an American to be the first one to cross the continent.

Ledyard actually made it to Siberia before Empress Catherine the Great had him arrested and sent back to Poland. The vision would lie dormant until Lewis and Clark—with a well planned, well funded, and superbly led expedition—went up the Missouri, over the Rockies, and down the Columbia to the Pacific. While the expedition faced starvation, hostile Native Americans, and ten-foot-deep snow, only one man died during the journey. Lewis was wounded but not by Native Americans, as one might suppose. Rather, he was shot in the backside by one of his own men who mistook him for a deer.

But I ask you, did Ledyard or Lewis and Clark have to contend with hostile powerboats? Here's what happens when I reach Brattleboro. Since the river is now loaded with powerboats and their wakes are battering my Old Town Pack canoe, I stay close to the New Hampshire side of the river for safety. As I pass by a dock, a powerboat cruises out and a water-skier hops into the water. I'm trapped between the shoreline and the boat, which is about to gun its engine to pull up the skier. Knowing the wake it produces could swamp me at such close range, I call, "Can you wait a minute till I get by?" The driver doesn't hear me or purposely ignores me. I call again, this time louder. He looks at me and gives the boat full throttle, jerking up the water-skier and sending an ocean-size wave my way.

I survive, but right then and there I decide to take a different approach to exploring the river. To avoid the few yahoos that think their motorboats make them macho, I'll paddle on weekdays or at dawn, avoiding the popular powerboat areas and enjoying those portions of the river valley by bicycle. It's clear the use of the river has changed as I approach Massachusetts. It's crazy to pretend I can have the Connecticut to myself as I did up north. I'm going to learn from the river, to go with the flow and adapt.

By the time I pull out at the launch site on Old Ferry Road in Brattleboro, a couple more motorboats have roared past, including a cabin cruiser the size of the *Love Boat*. While I'm putting the canoe onto the car, I fall into conversation with a boater who is launching his boat with twin engines. "Why is it," I ask, "that a small number of boaters seem to have it out for canoes?" "Well," he responded, "they just want to go fast and not change course drastically for a canoe. But most boaters will slow down and veer away from kayaks and canoes. I used to be one of the full-throttle boaters, until I hit a log; it was a close call that gave me religion."

I then ask him about the next couple of miles downriver to the Vernon Dam.

"You won't like it. Plenty of boats, and the river becomes lake-like behind the dam. The West River comes in on the Vermont side just above Route 119, and you might want to canoe up the river sometime to the Retreat Meadows Wildlife Area. But if I were you, I'd explore Brattleboro — it's a nice town — then check out the shad coming up the fish ladder at the Vernon Dam."

My powerboating friend is right about Brattleboro. It's a classic New England town with plenty of history. Walter Hard chronicles one tale about the town in *The Connecticut*. It involves an itinerant printer, named T. P. James, who had a strange experience while passing through Brattleboro. James claimed to have been visited by the spirit of the deceased Charles Dickens, and ordered to complete *The Mystery of Edwin Drood*, a book Dickens had only half finished when he suddenly died. The fact that James had never written anything before apparently didn't deter him. He labored for months in a secluded room in Brattleboro, churning out the second half of the manuscript. The book was eventually published, and fans of Dickens were amazed James could duplicate Dickens' style — they couldn't tell where one author ended and the other began.

Brattleboro's true literary hero, however, was Rudyard Kipling. He married Carrie Balestier who had spent summers at her grandmother's in Brattleboro. After they completed an around-the-world honeymoon, the couple visited Brattleboro in 1892 and purchased eleven acres in neighboring Dummerston. They soon began building a home, which they called Naulakha, an Indian word meaning *great treasure*. Naulakha was no ordinary home; it was built to be like a ship riding the crest of the hill, with Kipling's study in the bow. Here he wrote *Captain Courageous*, *The Jungle Book*, *Seven Seas*, and *A Day's Work*. Locals were impressed with having such a dignitary living in their midst, and knew how to make a buck: when Kipling wrote a check for goods, the recipient, instead of cashing it, would sell it to collectors for more than the amount indicated on the check. But what really drove Kipling out of Brattleboro was a feud with his brother-in-law, which escalated to the point where Kipling had him arrested for threats he made. The arrest didn't go over well with the locals and, when the negative publicity became unbearable, Kipling left Dummerston and

Wild turkeys, which can move quite quickly, head through a field toward the river.

Brattleboro for good in 1896. (Naulakha has since been restored by the Landmark Trust, a British organization that allows vacationers to rent the building.)

Just downstream from Brattleboro is the Vermont Yankee Nuclear Power Plant, situated on the banks of the river. It is a boiling-water reactor, which heats water to produce steam for generating electricity. The heat is a result of nuclear fission. Neutrons collide with the atoms of the uranium fuel in the reactor core, causing them to split and release more neutrons.

The steam created by the boiling water powers the turbine, which spins a generator and produces electricity. I always wondered why nuclear power plants were located on rivers and learned they use river water for cooling purposes. An intake structure at the river's edge admits water to the plant's condensers to cool the steam after it leaves the reactor. Literature from the power plant says that the Connecticut River water becomes heated after it cools the steam. In winter months this heated water is sent back to the river, where the additional heat is dissipated. During the summer months the heat in the water is dissipated into the air through two sets of mechanical draft cooling towers before being released to the river.

Whatever large-scale method we use to generate power has its concerns: hydroelectric dams block the river's flow and anadromous fish; the burning of fossil fuels creates air pollution and greenhouse gases; and nuclear power plants have the remote but potentially cataclysmic chance of an accident. Our efforts should be directed toward consuming less and using alternative sources to generate power, such as solar energy.

Just beyond the Vermont Yankee Nuclear Power Plant is the Vernon Dam, with a viewing window at the fish ladder that is quite entertaining. The fish ascend the ladder by first going up twenty-six steplike pools, each a foot higher than the preceding one, then through twenty-five vertical slot pools, each six inches higher than the preceding one.

While I was there in the spring, I saw equal numbers of lamprey eel and shad going by. While I was looking through the window, an eel came up and latched onto the glass, giving me a close-up view of its incredibly grotesque mouth.

Besides the viewing window, another window is open to the public — the site of one of the most unusual jobs I've come across. Inside a dark, cavernous room is a professional fish counter, tallying each species of fish that swims past the window. He told me, "So far today I've got about fifty shad, thirty lamprey, and one smallmouth."

"What about salmon?" I asked.

"None today," he said. "For the whole year, only four salmon have come by compared to 2,500 shad. Down at Holyoke, they have had 16,900 shad and fifty-seven salmon. Most of the salmon are removed at Holyoke for breeding purposes and about 10 percent are allowed to continue upstream on their own."

I ask about canoeing downstream from the dam.

"I see people do it, sometimes camping at Stebbins Island about a mile downstream. The next take-out isn't until about eight miles down in Massachusetts."

I shake my head. Not today. I've already got a plan to tour the next portion of river as a passenger.

8

Massachusetts Border to Turners Falls, Massachusetts

New Englanders are lucky souls because, no matter what direction we turn, we have water. I couldn't imagine living in the Southwest where there is no ocean, and few ponds and lakes. Even in Florida you can't swim in the lakes and rivers, unless you like alligators and warm, muddy water. Here in New England, especially in the northern three states, you can dive into just about any river, stream, lake, or pond for a cool dip.

I'm drawn to water, and this need has often influenced which road I've taken in the journey of life. When I left Saint Michael's College in Vermont for a great job in Chicago, I lasted all of eleven months. Why? Because I missed the hills of home and the clear flowing rivers and streams. When I returned to New England, the first thing I did was buy a ramshackle cabin in Vermont; not because the cabin was what I wanted, but because it overlooked a secluded pond. And it was a river that started me on my writing career. *Exploring The Hidden Charles* was first published eleven years ago. I've now come full circle, writing about the Connecticut River where I spent so many carefree summer days as a boy growing up in Longmeadow, Massachusetts.

Over the years, my fishing passion has waned a bit, but it's been replaced by a simpler sport. I can't seem to pass a river or lake without jumping in for a swim. There's something sensual about the softness of the water on your skin, the way it refreshes and relaxes. But, most of all, plunging into a cold river or lake makes you feel alive, the way you felt when you were a ten-year-old. I've taken this love of water to extremes, diving into a pond on a unseasonably warm day in December just to say I did it. Sure, I'm a fool, but love makes you do crazy things. I love to skinny dip, love to dive to the bottom of waterfalls to see the trout, love to float down rivers in an old pair of sneakers, and love to float on my back watching the spires of spruce trees meet blue sky and sailing clouds. Taking a dip at dawn is pure joy, as is an evening swim when a lake's surface is as smooth as polished stone. A quiet breaststroke makes me feel like I belong to the lake as much as the fish that fin silently below.

I spend a hot summer day floating down the Connecticut and Deerfield Rivers on my back, using a mask and snorkel to peer occasionally below. I know I make a strange sight, floating downriver while others are canoeing, but being in the water allows me to get one step closer to Mother Nature.

❖   ❖   ❖

As the Connecticut crosses the border out of Vermont and New Hampshire and into Massachusetts, no sign announces the change, but the river has now flowed 278 miles with 132 more to go. The river is wide and calm, but studded with plenty of powerboaters who launch from the Pauchaug Brook Boat Ramp in Northfield, which is also the northernmost end of the Pioneer Valley. Northeast Utilities has a picnicking and camping area with boat access downriver at the old Munn's Ferry Crossing. Below that is one of the larger islands in this stretch, Kidds Island, followed by the intake/outlet for Northfield Mountain Pumped Storage Hydroelectric Plant. Water is pumped from the river to the top of Northfield Mountain, where it plunges 850 feet through a pressure shaft to the turbine, generating power. (A few years ago this was proposed as the site to pump water from the Connecticut and divert it into Quabbin Reservoir to meet Boston's ever-growing needs. I'm happy to say that Boston's plan to tap the Connecticut River was dropped because of a concerted local effort.)

I've got the canoe on the car and river map in hand, but after swimming and free-floating down the Deerfield, I don't feel like working up a sweat by paddling. I decide to be lazy and tour the river from the deck of the *Quinnetukut II*, a tour boat run by Northeast Utilities that departs from their facility. The boat has a canopy, seats sixty people, and looks something like a large-scale *African Queen*. Instead of Humphrey Bogart and Katherine Hepburn at the wheel, we have a guide who narrates the cultural and natural history of the next twelve miles of the Connecticut. About a mile from our launch we pass by an enormous rock known as French King Rock. Most of the rock is submerged, but it does create turbulence. Before Turners Falls Dam was built the rock stood sixteen feet above the river. The rock, numerous powerboats, the quick water of French King Gorge ahead, and the tricky confluence at the

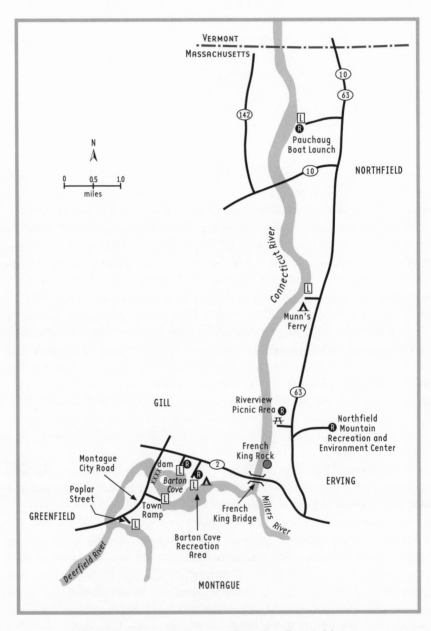

MASSACHUSETTS BORDER TO TURNERS FALLS, MASS.

upcoming Millers River are four reasons why paddlers should opt for the tour boat instead of a canoe.

There doesn't seem to be any one single explanation of how the rock got its name, but there is no connection with the Native American leader King Philip. One story I read said that during the French and Indian War a French soldier named the rock while on raid down the river.

A half-mile from the rock is the French King bridge, spanning the river between Erving and Gill. Several times I've strolled the sidewalk on the massive bridge, gazing down at the gorge and northward up the river into the hills of Vermont. Other times I've looked southward, watching the turbulent waters of the Millers River bring silt into the Connecticut. Now, in the water directly underneath, I see the inner guts of the three-span, steel rib arched bridge, and marvel that its construction was completed in just six months in 1932. It rises 140 feet and stretches 700 feet over the river in dramatic fashion. The arch of the bridge was something of a magnet for daredevil pilots who would illegally fly their planes beneath it.

Sculptured eagles adorn the lamps on the bridge, and a boater also has the chance to see some real eagles in the area. At Barton Cove, an impoundment above the Turners Falls Dam, bald eagles nest on Barton Island. The eagles who originally nested here in 1990 are thought to have come from the Quabbin Reservoir; the first nesting eagles since the bird was extirpated from Massachusetts because of hunting, loss of habitat, and the harmful effects of pesticides. I've seen only one eagle on the river in Massachusetts, but oh, what a sight, with its massive wingspan and distinctive white head. Their primary food is fish, which they will either snatch with their claws from the water or from another bird such as an osprey. They are accomplished scavengers, feeding on carcasses left by other animals. Great blue herons avoid building nests near bald eagles, knowing the eagle might swoop down on their nest and grab one of their young.

At the west end of Barton Cove is the dam at Turners Falls. The first dam at this location was built in 1798 to supply water for navigation in a canal that passed the falls. The present dam is used to generate electric power and the portage around it is three miles long! One of the reasons for such a long portage (all the way from the town ramp in Turners Falls to the primitive Poplar Street access) is that the water that used to flow through the riverbed below the dam is mostly diverted to the canal for industrial use. The riverbed can be dangerous. At times of high water, heavy rains, or runoffs, water can be released, and, therefore, paddlers should avoid the entire three miles below the dam. (Northeast Utilities will shuttle canoes and kayaks, but they usually need a three-day notice.) Canoeing is not allowed in the canal.

Most New Englanders have no idea how Turners Falls got its name, but the story is quite dramatic. During King Philip's Indian War (1675–76) there was one battle or massacre after another in this region, culminating with the English attacking the Native Americans at Turners Falls. The Battle of South Deerfield was the first of the bloody encounters, which occurred in the early days of the war on August 25, 1675 near Mount Sugarloaf. The colonists living in the region feared the local Norwottock might be incited by Wampanoag sachem Metacom (King Philip) and take to the warpath against the English settlers. Captains Lathrop and Beers were ordered by the authorities to surprise and disarm the Norwottocks. As Lathrop and Beers made their way to the Norwottock camp at Mount Sugarloaf, the Native Americans became aware of the approaching soldiers and fled into the nearby Hopewell Swamp. Here a three-hour

The French King bridge rises 140 feet and stretches 700 feet over the river in dramatic fashion. It was built in just six months in 1932.

fight ensued, killing nine English and approximately twenty Native Americans. The casualty count might suggest an English victory, but historian Eric Schultz, co-author of *King Philip's War,* thinks the real result of the battle "was to turn the neutral Norwottocks into deadly enemies."

The English quickly suffered two disasters after this brief battle. On September 2, 1675 in Northfield (called Squakeag at the time) natives reduced most of the town to ashes, killing eight settlers who were unable to make it to the safety of the garrison. Northfield was the northernmost settlement and the besieged settlers would have to be saved quickly and the town evacuated. Captain Beers was dispatched from Hadley to rescue those in the garrison and lead them south to safety. But Beers made the fateful mistake of approaching the town on the usual path along the high plain near the Connecticut River. What happened next is described in *History of the Town of Northfield*, written by authors J.H. Temple and George Sheldon: "This was the common route of travel at the time and the Indians knew that, as a matter of course, he [Captain Beers] would take it, and made their plans accordingly. Concealed in front, and behind the steep bank below the crossing-place, on his right, they fired upon the carelessly advancing column just as the head was passing the brook, when it would have been exposed for its entire length." Today a marker on the east side of Route 63 indicates the site of the ambush. Beers and his men made a stand, fighting and retreating southward, but the Native Americans won the battle, killing twenty-one English soldiers. Sixteen soldiers eventually made it back to Hadley, one straggled in six days later having covered himself with leaves and hidden in a gully. (This ravine is located adjacent to the Connecticut River, just west of Beers Hill, and is known as the Old Soldier Hole.) The besieged settlers huddled inside the Northfield garrison were not rescued until September 6, 1675 by Major Robert Treat and one hundred soldiers, who passed the grisly remains of Beers' men, some of whom had their heads stuck on poles.

After the disaster of Captain Beers' troops one might think the English would take all precautions against ambush, but on September 18 in South Deerfield, the Native Americans laid a successful trap. The victims were Captain Lathrop and a large body of troops, who were sent by the authorities to bring the Deerfield grain harvest south to the relative safety of Northampton and Hadley. Lathrop and his men left Hadley and headed north to Deerfield. They arrived without incident and loaded the wagons with grain. Perhaps this lulled them into a false sense of security. On the way back south some of the soldiers tired of carrying their heavy muskets and laid them in the carts atop the grain, while others stepped off the path to pick grapes. Upon arriving at a brook (now named Bloody Brook for what transpired) the soldiers began to cross the water. War-whoops erupted from the woods followed by a barrage of musket fire and a fusillade of arrows. Seventy soldiers and teamsters were killed, turning the brook red with their blood. (You may view the site on Main Street in

South Deerfield about three-quarters of a mile west of the Connecticut River.)

With disasters like this occurring with such frequency, the English were in jeopardy of abandoning all the towns along the Connecticut River in Massachusetts Bay Colony. Yet the settlers tenaciously defended the towns below Deerfield, though Hatfield and Springfield were attacked.

The natives may have won some early battles, but they were suffering as many casualties as the English, if not more. In a war of attrition this would slowly play against the Native Americans, whose population in New England was actually less than the English. Both sides staggered into the spring battles, but the Native Americans were facing starvation, and their need to catch fish was especially crucial since they were unable to grow crops the previous summer. Turners Falls was one such place where they gathered to catch shad and salmon. It was here they let their guard down, as the English had done so many times, leaving themselves exposed to surprise attack.

In the spring of 1676 two English captives escaped from the large Native American camp at the falls and relayed to Captain Turner, who was stationed in Hadley, that the camp was not well protected. Turner petitioned Connecticut Colony to send reinforcements so he could launch a raid on the camp, but Connecticut balked. Turner decided he couldn't wait any longer, and with 150 mounted volunteers from the surrounding river towns, he headed north along the river on the night of May 18. By dawn on May 19 they had reached the Native American camp, quietly circling around to the high ground to the north.

When Turner and his men suddenly stormed the camp, the Native Americans shouted "Mohawks, Mohawks!" thinking the charging soldiers were their longtime enemies from the west. Native Americans were shot in their wigwams, while others were slain running for the woods. A few natives made it to the banks of the Connecticut, jumped in canoes, and furiously paddled for the safety of the southeast bank. But the swollen spring waters were too much for the canoes, and the Native Americans who were not hit by musket balls were swept over the falls and dashed on the rocks below. The camp was set on fire and Native American women and children were indiscriminately killed in the destruction.

A period account from an unknown contemporary in Samual Drake's *Old Indian Chronicle* describes the attack as follows: "Our soldiers got thither after an hard march just about break of day, took most of the Indians fast asleep, and put their guns even into their wigwams, and poured in their shot among them, wherupon the Indians that durst and were able did get out of their wigwams and did fight a little (in which fight only one Englishman was slain) others of the Indians did enter the River to swim over from the English, but many of them were shot dead in the waters, others wounded were therein drowned, many got into canoes to paddle away, but the paddlers being shot, the canoes overset with all therein, and the stream of the River being very violent and swift in the place near the great falls, most that fell over board were borne by the strong current of the River, and carried upon the falls of water from those exceeding high and steep rocks, and from thence tumbling down were broken in pieces...."

The surprise attack might have been a total success had Turner left immediately and followed a well-planned exit strategy. But destruction of the encampment took time, allowing surviving warriors to regroup and gather on Turner's escape route. Only a few miles from the camp, at the Green River, the retreating Turner was shot and killed and his men fled in disarray. The counterattack by the Native Americans might have been even more effective had not Captain Holyoke rallied the terrified troops. He led them slowly southward in a defensive retreat along the Connecticut River, the Native Americans harassing them all the way to Hatfield. Thirty-nine soldiers never made it to Hatfield, but without Holyoke's command they all might have been lost.

In the end the loss for the Native Americans was far greater. The ambush at Turners Falls seems to have demoralized the natives, not only in the Connecticut River valley, but throughout Massachusetts and Rhode Island. In the next three months starvation and the knowledge of the war being lost caused Native Americans either to give up or to flee north, joining with the Abenakis who had risen up against the English on the Maine coast. Metacom returned to his homeland at Mount Hope, Rhode Island, and after more fighting was killed in an ambush.

Peace returned to the Connecticut River and settlers rebuilt Deerfield, but the Native Americans were not finished. In the late 1600s and the first part of the 1700s, Deerfield and towns along the river in Vermont and New Hampshire would be attacked repeatedly by Native Americans who had aligned themselves with the French. The peaceful river we know today was anything but peaceful 300 years ago. In 1704, a large force of French and Native Americans surprised the town of Deerfield, and once again the town was burned and forty-nine were killed. Even more remarkable is the number taken captive: 112. Since the attack occurred in February you can imagine the suffering of these captives as they were marched up the river and through Vermont to Canada. Twenty-one prisoners didn't make it, but most of those who did were eventually ransomed for their freedom.

❖   ❖   ❖

I wondered why the settlers risked their lives, knowing such isolated towns were targets of Native American attacks. Then I saw the farms and fields and knew the answer: the extraordinarily fertile soil in the lowlands made it perfect for agriculture. Where else could settlers get free land of

*Because Mount Sugarloaf stands alone over the valley,
the view from the summit is fantastic.*

such exceptional quality? Corn, potatoes, and onions are crops still grown here today. Even tobacco made a limited comeback with the popularity of cigar smoking. Hanging in the barns, the broadleaf tobacco used to wrap cigars has a familiar, welcoming look to me. Growing up in the valley, tobacco farms seemed to be everywhere, and many high school kids toiled in the fields on summer vacation.

The back roads of Montague, Deerfield, Sunderland, Whately, Hatfield, and Hadley have retained their rural heritage. One of my favorite drives is along River Road, starting in Hatfield and heading north into Whately and South Deerfield. I love the way Mount Sugarloaf juts up from the flat valley, looking more like a butte out west than a small mountain in New England. From River Road it appears to be vertical rock, but a road does reach the summit and is open seasonally. Because it stands alone over the valley, the view from the summit is fantastic. If you see a picture of the Connecticut winding through farmland, chances are it was taken from Mount Sugarloaf. (I've researched two different versions of how the mountain got its name. The first comes from days gone by when sugar was made into cone-shaped loaves, from which chunks could be carved as needed. The second version notes that the rock of the mountain is comprised of a Sugarloaf arkose variety of rock that runs through much of the valley. Chances are the mountain's name dates back long before the naming of the rock and, therefore, is named for the colonial cone-shaped pieces of sugar.)

Like most mountains in New England, Sugarloaf once had a hotel at the top, but in March of 1966 it caught fire and firefighters were unable to reach it because of snow. Mount Sugarloaf is the southernmost hill on the Pocumtuck Range, which runs north from Sugarloaf to where the Deerfield River joins the Connecticut. (On the other side of the Deerfield River another hill rises up, with the Poet's Seat Tower overlooking the Connecticut in Greenfield.)

The town just below Sugarloaf on the opposite side of the river is Sunderland, which has a unique roadside curiosity: a giant sycamore tree. Rising above Route 47 on the north side of the town center, it dwarfs passing cars and begs you to stop, look up at its gray- and brown-mottled branches, and be humbled. The sign underneath the tree says it has been living here since the signing of the Constitution in 1787. It is thought to be the largest sycamore east of the Mississippi, and anyone paddling the Connecticut should stop by and pay their respects.

Another place to pay your respects is farther up River Road in South Deerfield at one of the region's more forlorn-looking cemeteries. Pine Nook Cemetery rests on a windswept knoll and, like Sugarloaf, conjures up the image of a scene out of the western prairies. You half expect a tumbleweed to stop by. I usually stop at one particular grave because of the wake-up-call inscription on its headstone. It reads, "How soon this dream of life is over...we linger but a moment here."

9

MONTAGUE, MASSACHUSETTS, TO SUNDERLAND, MASSACHUSETTS

Since the first few miles of the river in Massachusetts had an abundance of powerboats, I wondered if any section was worth kayaking or canoeing. Thanks to a few farsighted individuals, a twelve-mile stretch, known as the Connecticut River Water Trail, is still perfect for paddlers. Motor restrictions of 15 MPH apply, and personal watercraft are banned from Montague to the boat launch in Hatfield. (An added deterrent to fast speeds and big boats is the area's shallow depth and many shifting sandbars.)

Much of the credit for this peaceful stretch of river goes to Terry Blunt, the Connecticut Valley Action program manager with the Massachusetts Department of Environmental Management. Blunt told me the speed restrictions on this twelve-mile stretch of river are not only for the benefit of paddlers, but to protect rare and endangered aquatic species like shortnose sturgeon.

Blunt has been advocating environmental protection of the Connecticut since 1970, when he arrived in New England after working with The Nature Conservancy in California and Washington. He immediately grasped the potential of the Connecticut, and his first position was director of the Connecticut River Watershed Council. His efforts on behalf of the river are far-reaching; from protecting open space along its banks to helping create the Norwottock Rail Trail—a recreation path spanning the Connecticut at Northampton and Hadley and running eastward for thirteen miles.

When I called Terry, asking advice about launch sites for this book, he never mentioned his accomplishments. I had no idea who he was except that he was helpful and seemed to know the river like the back of his hand. It wasn't until later I learned the river might look a lot less appealing today if Terry hadn't arrived thirty years ago. Karl Meyer, a naturalist with the Northfield Mountain Environmental Education Center, said it best: "If I were this river valley, Terry Blunt is the person I'd choose to have on my side."

From that original phone call to Terry, I learned about the primitive launch site on Poplar Street in Montague, and the twelve-mile run down the Connecticut that has become my favorite stretch south of the Sumner Falls/Cornish, New Hampshire area. Like most things, the first time I floated here was my favorite.

❖ ❖ ❖

Ed and I launch on a fine June day with blue sky above and clear water below. We can see shad racing upstream, leaping where small rapids impede their progress. We cast every fly and every lure in our tackle box to no effect. What I'd give for a shad dart, I say, thinking back on the lure that worked so effectively when I was growing up on the river in Longmeadow.

Ed tells me not to give up so easily. "Let's beach the canoe and wade out to that really fast stretch; we'll get one," he says.

It's worth a try and I slowly make my way across waist-deep water to a narrow channel, where I see the occasional flash of swimming shad. (Because I have not brought my waders, I strip down to my underwear; a far cry from the perfectly outfitted Orvis angler that Ed has become.) Watching the current glittering in the sun is hypnotic, and I don't mind casting again and again into the passage. Then something hits my leg and I look down to see a dark, snakelike object slither right between my bowed legs! I let out a scream and Ed wheels around from his casting position just in time to see me do a little jig. A two-foot-long lamprey eel has passed a little too close for comfort.

We continue fishing and Ed catches a nice smallmouth. I get nothing. I've got one eye on the water directly in front of me. Standing in the river in your underwear with eels cruising by is a little unsettling.

We hop back into the canoe and continue downriver. In some stretches the water is only a foot and a half deep; in others it seems to average five feet; and in a few spots deep holes, one angler told me, reach a depth of thirty-five feet. The river seems to be teeming with life — in all the shallow spots we see shad and lamprey.

"Careful of the big rock ahead," I warn from the bow.

We glide by and the rock moves; it's two monstrous fish with fins out of the water, each at least three feet long. The current, however, is so fast we can't get a good look at them, and what kind of fish they are God only knows—could be carp, sturgeon, or channel catfish.

Seeing the giant fish reminds me of all the strange aquatic monster sightings recorded in New England lakes and rivers. The earliest documented sighting was from none other than Samuel de Champlain in 1609. With Native American guides he entered Lake Champlain and chronicled seeing a five-foot-long serpent with silver-gray scales. "The point of the snout is like that of a hog," writes Champlain. "The fish makes war on all others in the lakes and rivers and possesses, as these people assure me, a wonderful instinct: which is, that when it wants to catch any birds, it goes among the rushes or reeds bordering the lake in many places, keeping the beak out of water without budging, so that when the birds perch on his beak, imagining it a limb of a tree, it is so subtle that closing the jaws which it keeps half open, it draws the birds under water by the feet. The Indians gave me a head of it, which they prize highly saying, when they have a headache they let blood with the teeth of this fish at the seat of the pain which immediately goes away."

The Connecticut River has had its share of strange sightings. Just recently kayakers coming downriver in Montague noticed something moving upstream, making a wake in front of them. They estimated it was five feet across. While they did not get a close look at it, my guess is it was a snapping turtle. Although the largest snapping turtles in the river are approximately thirty-six inches across, the water might have magnified the size of whatever they were seeing. Experts think a snapping turtle that large would be 250 to 300 years old. If it was a snapping turtle, remind me never to skinny-dip again.

❖ ❖ ❖

When we reach Third Island, we stretch our legs and explore a bit. Third Island is part of the Silvio O. Conte National Fish and Wildlife Refuge and overnight camping is not permitted. The interior of the island looks like a jungle of head-high ferns, brush, and vines.

Rather than bushwack back through the woods to Ed, I climb down the bank, using grapevines as handholds, and walk the island's shoreline. No tracks are in front of me and I have that Robinson Crusoe feeling of being the first person to tread here. It truly is a perfect day: cobalt blue skies, no humidity, and a gentle breeze drifts down from the north. A few puffy, white cumulus clouds with flat bottoms dot the horizon. Birds come and go, killdeer scurry along the shoreline, a kingfisher screeches at me, and an osprey floats overhead.

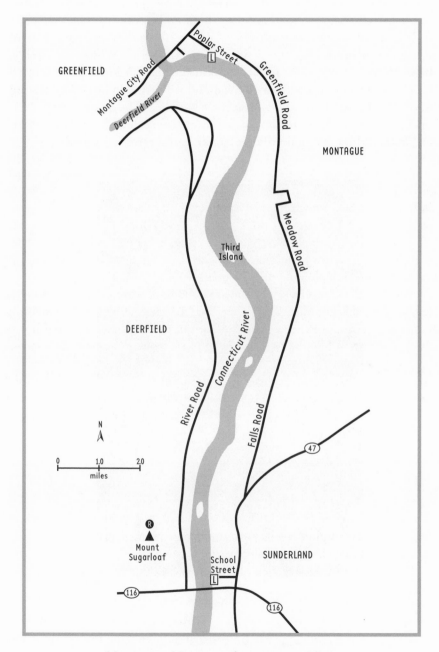

MONTAGUE, MASS., TO SUNDERLAND, MASS.

When I see Ed I shout, "Remember last winter? These are the days we dream about."

We paddle some more and I marvel that we are in heavily populated Massachusetts. Because the banks are high and mostly wooded, we have not seen a single sign of civilization. I've read that on the west side of the river south of Clapp Brook is an area known as Whitmore's Ferry, where Jurassic-period fish-fossil beds can be seen in low water. But Ed is catching smallmouth with his fly rod and we forget to look. His casting ability is far better than mine and so is his patience. The quiet, almost Zen-like concentration of fly-fishing seems to fit this secluded stretch of river, and I'm thankful once again that personal watercraft are banned.

Sunderland can be seen clearly from the top of Mount Sugarloaf.

Soon the rust-colored sandstone cliffs of Mount Sugarloaf can be seen to the west. (There are actually two peaks, North and South, to the Sugarloaf Mountains, although everyone calls the southern peak with the distinctive reddish cliffs Mount Sugarloaf.) We pass another large island, Second Island, before floating the last three miles to the Sunderland Bridge. The day's paddle is one I won't soon forget. Here's the best part: I don't have to canoe, hitchhike, or bicycle back upstream to my car—Ed's truck is waiting for us at the School Street launch.

❖ ❖ ❖

That night we camp to the west, up the Deerfield River at Mohawk Trail State Forest. I arise early, but Ed is already off fishing the Deerfield, so I grab a couple of granola bars, an apple, and my water bottle and start climbing the south side of Todd Mountain. The path is steep but well shaded by oak, ash, and maple, with mountain laurel growing thickly in the understory. This trail and the one running along the ridge top are in the exact same spot as the original Native American path, now called the Mohawk-Mahican Trail. (The steep trail would have had little effect on Native Americans who often covered fifty miles in a single day. The original Mohawk-Mahican trail took the most direct route west, from New York State to the Connecticut River, and didn't worry about steep grades as modern-day roadways must consider.)

It's about an hour to the top but the view to the east is a nice reward. This section of the Berkshires is like the Continental Divide; the Cold and Deerfield Rivers below me feed the Connecticut River, but the rivers to the west flow toward New York. Not another soul has ventured to the mountain top and I have the summit to myself. At the campground several signs explain that black bears live in these forests, and I figure I have an outside chance of seeing one. But the woods are still, and a lone turkey vulture, circling in a thermal updraft, is all the wildlife I see. Still, the mountain has much to offer, particularly the north side with one of New England's best remaining patches of old-growth forest.

Old-growth forests exist on land never logged or disturbed by humans. Such trees are not necessarily the tallest. Often times trees older than 250 years are stunted, growing on steep, rocky terrain and facing the full force of the wind and elements, like the north side of Todd Mountain. Although settlements existed in the Berkshires in the mid-1700s, forest cutting at that time would have focused on clearing the better agricultural land and harvesting timber in accessible places.

I retrace my steps across the ridge and this time descend the mountain on the north side, stopping to admire the hemlock. Some have a bonsai appearance; gnarled, twisted, and relatively small but still over 200 years old. I look at the rings on a fallen tree that had been cut and can see, after the first few years of quick growth, the rings narrowed considerably to tiny fractions of an inch.

Good views of the red cliffs of Mount Sugarloaf can be seen both from the south and the north on the river.

Farther down the north side I remember a section of trail I once hiked with old-growth tree expert Bob Leverett. I follow the trail he recommended and come to New England's tallest sugar maple. Situated in a grove of tall pine and ash trees, it is difficult to appreciate the full scale of its 105-foot height. I remember Leverett said to try and picture the sugar maple next to a house out in a field, and immediately I grasp its grandeur. Nearby is a ninety-five-foot-tall maple, which a hiker might assume is another sugar maple, but is actually a red maple, growing far beyond its average fifty-foot height.

Perhaps the most impressive trees are at the base of the mountain where the Indian Pines, two incredibly tall white pines, tower 150 feet above the trail. The trees are among the tallest white pines in New England and are named after two Mohawk leaders: the Jake Swamp Tree and the Joe Norton Tree. (A handsome carved sign, made by Mohawk Trail State Forest park assistant supervisor Chuck Bellows, lets the public know they have reached this special spot.)

10

SUNDERLAND, MASSACHUSETTS, TO HATFIELD, MASSACHUSETTS

My eight-year-old son Brian sits in the front of the canoe, one hand hanging over the side, making sweeping motions in the water. We've been on the water all of five minutes and he's asking if we are near the swimming spot yet. No, I tell him, we are saving that for later. Wanting him to love the river as I do, our first outing will be a short one, starting at the Sunderland Bridge and ending at the public boat launch in Hatfield. I've also made it easy on Dad, bringing along the electric motor to supplement the paddling.

We paddle the first mile, trolling our fishing line behind us. How many times, I wonder, have I taken Brian fishing and caught nothing. I desperately want him to love this bittersweet sport, so we have an activity we can always do together. At home his interests are already curving away from mine; he gravitates toward playing and watching team sports and I'm more into outdoor recreation. But he does seem to enjoy the river, and when he asks if we can stop paddling and use the motor, I don't hesitate.

As soon as the propeller comes to life, we get a strike on one of the rods. It becomes clear the bass prefer the lures to move fast, and I remember the fish Ed caught on the last trip struck when we were both paddling. Casting to the banks, which usually works, wasn't nearly as effective as trolling at fast speeds.

I pass the rod to Brian, though I'm afraid it's going to be yanked out of his hands. Way behind the boat a good-size smallmouth bass jumps, and I tell Brian to hold on as tightly as he can with one hand and reel in the line with the other. When he's got the fish near the canoe, it makes a last dive and the rod wraps around the side of the canoe. The line goes slack and I think we've lost the fish until it explodes from the water, sending a spray of water on Brian.

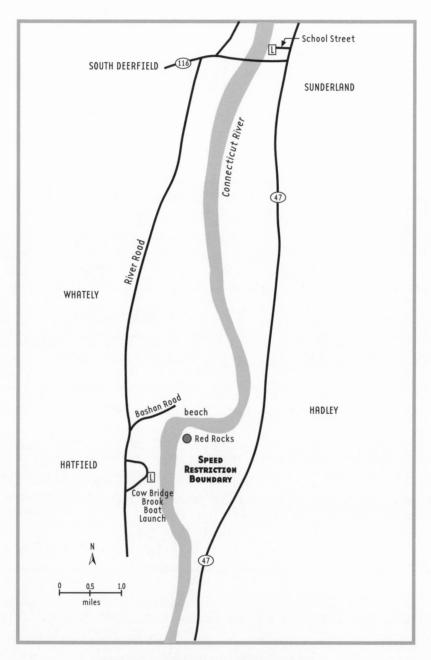

SUNDERLAND, MASS., TO HATFIELD, MASS.

Luckily I've got a net and I'm able to dip it beneath the tired small-mouth and bring it in. I snap a picture, capturing the excitement in the face of an eight-year-old upon landing his first big fish. We release the smallmouth and watch this beautiful bronze god from the deep shoot to the rocks below.

I recommend a day on the river for any parent who wants to get closer to a son or daughter. Or you could really go all out and spend several weeks on the river as Turk Leebaert did with his two sons during the summer of 1999. Leebaert, his sons Corky, thirteen, Timmy-Bruce, eleven, and family friend Jim Flanagan, all from Fairfield, Connecticut, took a unique approach to floating the river: they built an old-fashioned flatboat and began a source-to-sea trip. The wooden boat, named *The Restless*, was fifteen feet, complete with a cabin and four bunk beds. Powered solely by its crew, using oars and sails, the foursome found their progress impeded by frequent south winds blowing up the river, and often traveled by night when the winds subsided. Because of all the dams and low water, they also brought two vehicles to trailer *The Restless* around dams and shallows.

As the group made their way downriver, local newspapers interviewed the men and boys and I kept abreast of their progress. Leebaert made it clear his number one priority was to spend time with his children. In an interview in the *Daily Hampshire Gazette*, Leebaert said, "One of the messages of this trip is to spend a lot of time with your family, regardless of your condition and selfish desires. My most important job is being a parent. I'd rather lose any other job. You can get money from everywhere, but you can't get the love and respect of your kids unless you earn it. They'll only be this age once." Amen. Wouldn't it be great if we all had this attitude and put it into action?

Brian and I have it easy compared to rowing a flatboat. Besides the help of the little electric motor, the wind is from the north. We erect a sail by rigging a plastic garbage bag between our two paddles and I hold them upright. The gusts of wind are so strong, we find the sail works better than the motor and the canoe literally flies downriver. We have plenty of time to stop and fish along six small sandbars that are probably submerged during the spring. We catch another smallmouth there, this one hitting a small spinner.

Sailing downriver, it's hard to see over the twenty-foot banks separat-ing the water from the Pioneer Valley floodplain. Occasionally we can see a field, and I'm thankful it's cornstalks rather than roofs that reach toward the sky. (Even farmers' fields can pose a hazard to the river's health, particularly from the use of pesticides and herbicides to control insects and grubs, weeds and fungi. The U.S. Department of Interior reports that the herbicides most frequently detected in the agricultural stretches of the

Connecticut River are atrazine and metolachlor, both typically used for
weed control in the cultivation of feed corn.)

*My eight-year-old son, Brian, catches his first
smallmouth bass on the river.*

Only one powerboat passes us, going slowly because of the speed
restriction from Montague to Hatfield. The shallow depth of the river also
acts as a natural control on bigger boats, although in some spots the river is
deeper than I can thrust my paddle. In some places the river is only a foot or
two deep and is as clear as it was in northern Vermont. The lack of rain has
something to do with the water's clarity, but so does the lack of power boats:
the propeller from a large motor can stir up silt to a depth of twelve feet.

Farther downstream a powerboat streaks by, ignoring the speed
restriction and risking a serious accident. In fact, in 1999 a fatality
occurred downstream when two boats collided in Hatfield. The cause
of the accident is unclear, but on a river there isn't a lot of room for error.
Often times accidents are a result of boating under the influence of

alcohol, even though Massachusetts has stricter penalties than most states. (Operating a vessel with a blood alcohol level of .08 or more in Massachusetts can result in license revocation.) While the laws and penalties may be tough, I wonder about enforcement due to a lack of resources. Equally troublesome is that anyone sixteen or older can operate a motorboat, and even a twelve-year-old can operate one alone if he or she has completed an approved basic boating course. I know what I was like at fifteen and no one would have been safe for miles if I had had my own motorboat.

Brian and I continue sailing south until the river takes a turn to the west. Brian spots what he has been looking for all day—swimmers. On the western shore is a sandy beach, standing out in marked contrast to the soft, silted banks behind us. The beach is known as the Bashan, since it's located on Bashan Road, and quite a crowd has gathered.

Downstream, on the eastern side of the river is another, smaller, sandy beach; this one accessible only by boat. We paddle over and join three groups of people who have beached their powerboats and are taking turns hurling themselves into the river on an old-fashioned rope swing. It looks like great fun and we give it a go—Brian dropping from the rope about three feet up, I from four or five feet. Then a young daredevil takes the rope, climbs a tree, launches himself into the air, and lets go when he's about twenty feet above the water. For a moment I think of trying the same thing; then I realize I'm twice his age and half as limber.

The water is cool and feels great, and I think about how when I was growing up on the river no one in his or her right mind swam in it. Even now I wouldn't swim downstream from this point because a water treatment plant empties into the river, and further downstream the cities of Holyoke, Springfield, and Hartford are too close for comfort. I also avoid swimming in any stretch after heavy rains, which increase runoff and the possibility of sewer overflow.

During dry weather, from the Bashan northward, the river is generally clean. The Massachusetts Water Watch Partnership recently confirmed this fact. Their group of volunteers collected water samples from a dozen sites every two weeks between June and September. The results showed that during dry weather the river appeared to be clean enough to support all types of recreational use, including swimming.

After our swim we paddle downriver a short distance and head to the Cow Bridge Brook Boat Launch. There the speed restriction ends and the motorboat traffic is considerably greater. We cut our way across the wakes and haul the canoe out of the water. In a half-hour our ride will be here.

Right on schedule, Mike Callahan arrives and gives us a ride back to our car; we then follow him to Hadley. A year earlier Mike learned I was researching and paddling the river and sent me a note offering lodging at his inn, the Clark Tavern Inn Bed and Breakfast. The home is steeped in history but has all the modern comforts, including a pool, which Brian is swimming in before we even unload our suitcase. Then he's out of the pool, exploring the handsome garden, and shouts for me to come and see the fish. Swimming inside a large garden pool are fish of every color, and Brian has their full attention as he throws them fish pellets supplied by Mike.

While Brian feeds the fish, Mike introduces me to his wife, Ruth, and we all enjoy a drink on the screened porch as the sun sets. "We looked along the coast of Maine to buy an inn," Ruth says, "but I just knew in my heart I wanted to stay in the valley. We love this place."

The Clark Tavern Inn was not always situated in Hadley, but was originally built in Northampton on the banks of the Connecticut River. Owned by Benjamin Alvord, it was sold in 1742 to Ezra Clark, who ran a tavern from the house and began operating a ferry between Hadley and Northampton. Historian Betty Allen, writing in *Early Northampton*, described the tavern's early days: "What joyous mugs of hot flip have been handed out from the old inn to shivering riders! What cooling decoctions of mint from the old garden have revived the wilted spirits of travelers in the stuffy stagecoach."

In its colonial heyday the Clark Tavern was the hub of local activity. The ferry carried all sorts of passengers—from livestock to General Burgoyne and his defeated redcoats on the way back to Boston. The 1800s ushered in the area's first bridge and the temperance movement; both ferry and tavern were soon closed. More than a century passed with the tavern as a private residence. In 1961 the Clark Tavern was scheduled to succumb to the wrecking ball, as it was in the proposed path of Interstate 91. Hadley residents Ted Johnson and John Brassord came to the rescue, purchasing the tavern, then disassembling and rebuilding it on the Hadley side of the river. Now the inn enjoys privacy and the sense of permanence that comes from the woodwork, the exposed beams, and the dozens of antiques.

❖   ❖   ❖

Over breakfast the next morning Mike Callahan tells me about his latest interest: beaver. Prior to the arrival of Europeans, the landscape was dotted with beaver dams, shallow ponds, and the slow-moving flowage the dams create. Beaver were spread throughout every watershed in North America except extreme desert areas and the lower part of what is now

Florida. Other than humans, beaver are one of the only animals to alter entire ecosystems to form their ideal habitats; building houses, canals, and dams while felling trees and storing food. Native Americans called them "the little people."

Once the Europeans arrived and the fur trade reached full swing, the beaver population was decimated, and by the time of the American Revolution, they had been extirpated from Massachusetts. In 1932 Morris Pell, a warden at Pleasant Valley Bird and Wildlife Sanctuary, reintroduced beaver into the Berkshires. That same year the beaver protection bill was passed and the state helped to establish the beaver population by live-trapping and relocating beaver throughout the Commonwealth. The population has climbed ever since.

In 1996 the beaver population really took off when Massachusetts residents voted to prohibit the use of body-gripping traps, such as the Conibear leg-hold traps used for beaver. Trappers stopped catching beaver because these inexpensive, lightweight traps were outlawed; the only alternatives were the large Bailey, Hancock, and Tomahawk landtraps, all of which cost about $275 each (compared to $10 for a Conibear trap). With adult beaver, which mate for life, having between four to six offspring a year, it's easy to see how an unchecked population could grow. Battle lines were drawn between those wanting the beaver population to grow without human interference and those who saw the burgeoning population as a threat to their property.

Mike and Ruth Callahan wondered if there were some middle ground to protect property without killing the beaver. They attended a Massachusetts Society for the Prevention of Cruelty to Animals (MSPCA) clinic about alternatives to killing beaver, such as installing new and improved flow pipes to keep beaver ponds from expanding to the point where they harm nearby roads or property. The MSPCA clinic launched Mike and Ruth's plan on behalf of the beaver. Mike and Ruth organized volunteers to install new flow devices.

"We quickly found many of the pipes in use were the old style that didn't work well," Mike explained. "We knew that the new flow devices worked much better. Our first challenge was a pond near the Connecticut River that was flooding the Norwottuck Rail Trail, a popular bike path that crosses the river. We installed one of the new devices, which has perforated openings where the water flows. Because beaver plug up openings in the dams by the sound and feel of running water, these pipes did not attract the beaver's attention because the release of water is slow and relatively quiet. And just in case the beaver did try, we also installed a three-foot-diameter cage around the pipe. The pipes worked great at the

Norwottuck Trail site, and now people can enjoy riding on the trail and watching the beaver."

To protect an individual tree from being felled by a beaver, a property owner can install a protective wire cylinder around the tree. Developed by the Beaver Defenders of Newfield, New Jersey, the cage is designed of heavy wire fencing with two inch by four inch openings extending three feet up the tree. The space between the cage and the tree should be about twelve inches, and it is important to secure the device to the ground to prevent beaver from crawling underneath.

"The more work we did," relates Mike, "the more I realized how important beaver are to the environment because of the new wetlands they create. They are a keystone species that benefit a wide diversity of wildlife, from the great blue herons that nest in the dead standing timber in the ponds to the turtles that sun themselves on the fallen logs. Half of our country's endangered species rely on wetlands for survival. Beaver-created wetlands are equal to the rain forests in the abundance of life they support." (Wetlands also function like a natural tub or sponge, storing water and slowly releasing it to help prevent flooding and erosion. Wetlands are crucial to some of Massachusetts' lesser known creatures, particularly reptiles and vertebrate animals; half of all the reptiles in the state are threatened.)

"I learned a lot," said Mike, "from Skip Lisle, a wildlife biologist for the Penobscot Nation up in Maine. He developed a device called the Beaver Deceiver, and that prompted me to experiment with flow pipes. We eventually constructed an inexpensive flow device that could be hidden under the water and in the dam. The Flexible Leveler is what we call it, and it works very well in watersheds of low to moderate flow. We use a perforated six-inch-diameter PVC pipe for inlets and connect that to a length of flexible, corrugated plastic pipe that is laid just beneath the top of the dam. A connection on the downstream side of the dam runs thirty feet, and the beaver do not try and plug it."

The true beauty of people like Mike and Ruth Callahan is that their efforts are without monetary reward. Their payoff is the satisfaction of protecting both the beaver and the wetlands, to the benefit of us all. We'd better wake up and address the larger problem: the overpopulation of our own species makes the number of beaver look small in comparison.

11

HADLEY, MASSACHUSETTS, TO HOLYOKE, MASSACHUSETTS

The river Brian and I enjoyed would not have been possible without the Connecticut River Watershed Council (CRWC), an organization that fights for improving and protecting water quality. Equally important is their effort to conserve natural and scenic resources, by protecting open space and advocating for reasoned land use. Even if a river is clean, how appealing can it be with few access points and banks lined by "Keep Out" signs? To this end, the CRWC has had solid success, protecting over 8,000 acres through their Land Conservation Program, while keeping access points public.

A week after my stay at the Clark Tavern, I visit the CRWC headquarters in Easthampton and learn about the Connecticut's recent designation as an American Heritage River, a national honor bestowed on only a handful of waterways. From a practical perspective, the designation will bring technical consulting assistance and possible funding from the federal government to aid communities and institutions in achieving environmental and cultural preservation goals. It enables local communities to access the help they need in working with federal agencies to carry out their projects. The Connecticut will even have its own river navigator, a federal agency employee who acts as an ombudsperson and knows how to get things done in Washington and Boston, where most agencies are headquartered.

The CRWC is also involved with the relicensing of the Connecticut's sixteen hydroelectric dams, which will come up for review by the Federal Energy Regulatory Commission (FERC) at various times over the next twenty years. The CRWC works to influence the FERC's review by advocating for less fluctuating of water levels above a dam, provisions for up- and downstream fish passage, protection of riverside lands, and facilities for public access and recreation. Equally important are their efforts to have a more consistent flow below the dams.

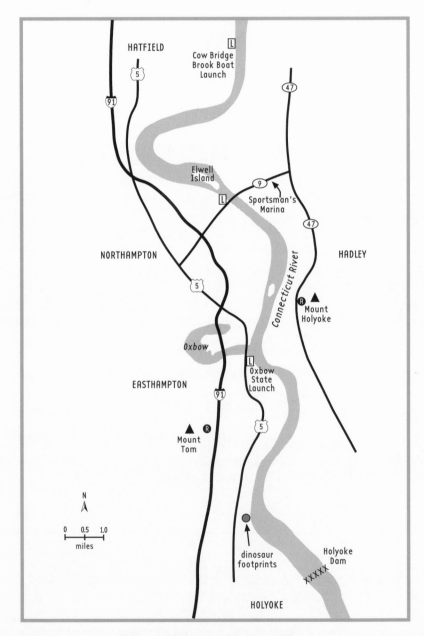

HADLEY, MASS., TO HOLYOKE, MASS.

Improving the dam's impact on anadromous fish goes hand in hand with the CRWC's overall efforts on river health, and in particular their support of returning Atlantic salmon to the river. But the salmon story to date has been one of frustration. There seem to be at least a dozen reasons why the salmon restoration program has not resulted in large-scale numbers of salmon migrating up the river. One hypothesis reasons that the salmon are being eaten by the striped bass in the lower part of the river. Another blames the hydropower turbines awaiting the salmon fry on their downstream passage. A particularly disturbing theory claims that global warming has affected the salmon, a species sensitive to even minor fluctuations in temperature. The river's increased numbers of gizzard shad, cousins of the American shad, seem to support the notion that the ocean is warming. The gizzard shad typically swim up more southern waterways, such as the Delaware, Chesapeake, and Mississippi, and were nonexistent in the Connecticut River prior to 1980. The Connecticut River itself has probably warmed in the last century from warm-water discharges into the river from industry and the cutting of shade trees, as well as from climate changes.

When the salmon restoration program started in 1961, officials estimated that thousands of salmon would be swimming up the Connecticut to spawn. Besides cleaning the river and introducing salmon smolt, fish passages were built around all the dams up to East Ryegate, Vermont. But to date, with the exception of one good year in 1981, fewer than 300 fish return each year, even though more than 150 million dollars has been spent on the program. A silver lining to the effort is that the improvement in fish passages have benefited the shad and herring, which are forage species for striped bass and salmon.

❖ ❖ ❖

While I'm at the CRWC headquarters, the staff assists me in locating old photographs of the river. Without a doubt, floods are the most photographed event on the river. Several yellowed prints show the river overflowing its banks, inundating farmland and whole neighborhoods. Most of the flood photographs were taken in September of 1938, the year of a killer hurricane.

The hurricane of 1938 devastated New England, like a similar one two years earlier. The state of Connecticut and the Pioneer Valley were particularly hard hit from the raging river. The eye of the hurricane came right up the Connecticut Valley, traveling from New Haven to Hadley in just two hours. The fast-moving storm was made even more deadly along the region's rivers, because it followed a week of rain that had saturated the ground. Six hundred eighty-two New Englanders were killed.

In Springfield, residents sandbagged the dike for reinforcement and it held. The south end, however, had no dike and was evacuated; 250 prisoners at the Hampden County Jail on York Street had to be moved to the gymnasium at Springfield College. The Eastern States Exposition in West Springfield was completely flooded, and the grandstand, Ferris wheel, and several buildings were blown over.

Chicopee was also devastated. The bridge at Chicopee Falls was swept away, taking the telephone lines with it. To establish communication between Chicopee and Springfield, the telephone company used artillery, brought up from Connecticut by a coast guard plane, to shoot a telephone line across the Chicopee River.

Hartford and several other Connecticut towns suffered massive flooding, as did the Berkshires; the Mohawk Trail was literally torn away by the Cold River. The Ware River decimated the mill town of Ware, leaving 600 people homeless, and the farming communities along the Connecticut, such as Hadley and Northampton, suffered total crop loss. Apple farms incurred long-term damage, losing the ripening crop of apples, and, as the storm increased in intensity, the trees themselves were uprooted by the wind.

❖   ❖   ❖

Dikes have been erected in some areas to prevent flooding and I spend an hour walking the dike in Hadley. The dike is best visited on the north side of the nearly one-mile-long town common, which intersects Route 9. (Many of the dikes built along the river from Hadley to Hartford were constructed right after the terrible flooding of 1936.)

The area by the Hadley common is susceptible to flooding because the river makes a big bend to the west just above the town common then curls back to the east just below it. If the river had a mind to save a mile or two and flow due south, it would follow the course of Route 47, cutting off the two miles of Hadley that fills this curve in the river. Who knows, maybe the river will eventually flow this way; dikes often fail as they did in the great flood on the Mississippi in 1993. Because we have built upon lowlands near the river, dikes have become necessary in places but they are certainly not natural. By channeling water in a more constricted area, without allowing it into the natural floodplain, the next town downstream without a dike gets clobbered twice as hard.

From the dike I drive north, explore such uniquely named back roads as Honey Pot Road, and poke around some old cemeteries like the one north of Hadley Common. Eventually I end up photographing a barn with tobacco leaves hanging inside. Mark Sadlowski wanders out and explains this is broadleaf tobacco used for wrapping cigars. Our conversation soon turns from farming to the river.

"I've scuba-dived in the river several times," explains Mark, "and have seen all sorts of things. Once I saw a five foot sturgeon, and lately I've been seeing small striped bass that come up with the shad. A friend of mine even found a seven foot anchor with a big spade in it, which looked like it came from a large ship. And when you paddle the river be sure to be on the lookout for the bald eagle; there has been one nesting here in Hadley where some high-tension lines cross the river."

Although Mount Holyoke isn't especially tall, it offers commanding vistas. The best view is of the Connecticut River to the north.

After visiting Mark's farm, I stop at Mount Holyoke. Although the mountain isn't especially tall, it offers a commanding vista as it rises abruptly from the lowlands, just as Sugarloaf does to the north.

Mount Holyoke is part of the Holyoke Range, a unique group of hills with an east-west orientation rather than the north-south direction of the Berkshires and most other mountain ranges in the region. Formed 200 million years ago when lava spilled forth from a crack in the earth's crust, the Holyoke Range is rich in iron and has oxidized to a dark reddish hue.

The best view is to the north, where the Connecticut River snakes through a checkerboard of green, yellow, and brown fields. Beyond the farmland to the east is Amherst and the University of Massachusetts; to the northwest is one of my favorite towns, Northampton. It was also a town much loved by Calvin Coolidge, who retired there at his handsome estate known as the Beeches, purposely shunning the attention that follows a former president. (When Coolidge filled out the form with his annual dues to the National Press Club, he put "retired" in the line for occupation and under remarks he added, "Glad of it.") Northampton was also the terminus for a seventy-five-mile-long canal starting in New Haven and built to bypass rapids and falls with its sixty locks. In 1835 the first boat was drawn up the canal by a team of horses, but due to poor construction and several years of drought, the canal stayed in operation for only twelve years.

To the southwest of Mount Holyoke is Mount Tom, and due west is one of the river's unique features: the Connecticut River oxbow at Northampton. Prior to 1841 the river flowed through this loop. During high water due to an ice jam, however, the river abandoned the bend to create a more direct downstream course, leaving the oxbow as a lake with a tiny outlet to the Connecticut. The new path shortened the river by three miles, and Hadley lost 400 acres to Northampton because the land was now on the west side of the river. The oxbow is the subject of a wonderful painting by Thomas Cole titled *View from Mount Holyoke, Northampton Massachusetts, After a Thunderstorm*. The painting, commonly referred to as the *Oxbow*, is a mix of contrasts; the foreground of Mount Holyoke is under the dark grip of the thunderstorm, but the valley below is bathed in warm sunlight.

As good as the scenery before me is, it's the house on top of the mountain that catches my attention. The Summit House (also known as the Prospect House) was built as a mountaintop inn in the early 1800s. What a grand place it must have been, perched above the valley floor. Guests were brought to the inn on a tramway, first powered by horses, then steam, and, later, electricity. Many other mountains in New England had similar mountaintop inns, but the Summit House is one of the few still standing. The Summit House is now publicly owned and is part of Skinner State Park. Best of all, visitors like myself can sit on the front porch and enjoy a bird's-eye view of the river, looking forward to their next river excursion.

❖ ❖ ❖

I've floated the river with friends, both brothers, and my son, so I figure it's time to make a trip with someone entirely different: Big Bill, a sidekick from elementary school. We lost touch over the years, but at a recent high school reunion we renewed our friendship. When he learned of my Connecticut River trips he expressed an interest in accompanying me, even though he'd never paddled a canoe.

"Well, I'm not going in any canoe," Big Bill booms. "It's total mayhem on the water. My brother and I rented a pontoon boat last year and the river was filled with crazy people, flying every which way in speed boats."

"What if we rent a small fishing boat with an outboard motor?" I ask.

"I guess we'll be safe in one of those. Ok, I'm in. I'll meet you at the Sportsman's Marina in Hadley at 1:00 P.M. on Friday. I'll be the one wearing a sombrero and clogs. I may even put on a Speedo."

I wonder if Big Bill can survive in a boat, away from civilization for five hours.

"Do you still stop at convenience stores every thirty minutes when you're not at home?" I ask.

"Don't worry about me, I'll be fine," he says. "Just bring the fishing rods; I want to see if you know what you're talking about in your newspaper column."

I make a mental note to bring the rods, plenty of snacks, and perhaps a flare gun. A trip with Big Bill—even one as tame as this—could be fraught with danger. Strange things happen to him. I could see us careening over the Holyoke Dam. The newspapers would report that all the police were able to find was a sombrero and a Speedo bathing suit.

On the day of our trip, I arrive at the marina in the morning, allowing plenty of time to become familiar with the boat before Big Bill boards. I've packed everything I can think of that he might possibly need: throat lozenges, cold capsules, Diet Cokes, candy bars, Twinkies, cashews, Gummy Bears, cigars, and plenty of sunscreen.

Marina owner, Gary Pelissier, tells me river otters are back on the Connecticut. "My friends have seen them, but so far I've only seen where they've been—right under my docks. Last fall when we pulled the docks out for the winter, there were mountains of empty mussel shells on the Styrofoam floats holding the dock up. The otters must have brought the mussels there to eat in a safe, hidden spot." Since the marina's establishment in 1955, the river and its ecosystem has changed constantly. "Every year I'm rewarded with a new sight. Last year a bald eagle and this year a whole cove was rippling with surfacing baby shad."

We walk down to the boat and he gives me a quick lesson in running the motor, reminding me of the channel buoys: keep the red ones on your right when facing upstream and the green on the left. The boat works like a charm and I head north to the Cow Bridge Brook Boat Launch in Hatfield where Brian and I pulled out a week earlier. How strange it feels to be going faster than three miles per hour, but I'm not complaining. A light drizzle is falling and the mountains are shrouded in fog—a perfect day to be on the river because I have it all to myself. I'm tempted to open the motor to full throttle, but after passing a whole tree partially submerged in the middle of the river, I think twice.

Once at the Hatfield launch I float back downriver at a slow pace, trolling my line in hopes of catching a smallmouth. When I reach Elwell Island, I stay to the broad, east side and catch my first bass, a ten inch smallmouth. (Canoeists will want to stay on the narrow, more secluded west channel.) Then it's under the Calvin Coolidge Bridge and back to the dock.

Big Bill is waiting in the rain wearing an Orvis fishing hat. Not trusting me to supply all the equipment, he has purchased a Zebco fishing rod and reel, still shrink-wrapped to the display box. He also has a brand new tackle box, filled with every assortment of rubber creepy crawler.

Once Big Bill is safely seated in the bow, I let the motor rip, figuring we have the river to ourselves. I want to give him a sense of the exhilaration I've enjoyed in the morning. At once his hat blows off and we spend the next ten minutes circling back, finally to snag it out of the water.

We slow to trolling speed off Rainbow Beach on the west side of the river and Big Bill has his first hit.

"I've got something!" he hollers.

But I notice there's no bend in his rod. "I don't think so."

"I'm sure of it. I've got a fish," he exclaims.

Then to my amazement a smallmouth jumps behind the boat with one of Big Bill's creepy crawlers hanging from its mouth.

Big Bill quickly reels the fish to the boat. "Now what?" he asks.

"Pick it up and bring it in. Just grab it by the lower jaw," I say.

"What about it's teeth? I'm sure it has teeth," he says.

"For crying out loud, just pick it up. It's only eight inches," I say.

Big Bill will have none of it, not wanting to risk a finger to the mighty jaws of a baby smallmouth. Instead, he swings the fish into the boat and it lands at my feet. We bicker like children over who will take it off the hook until we agree I'll unhook this one and Big Bill will handle the next.

We pass by the narrow exit from the Oxbow where I've been told boats can stack up like jets on a runway during summer weekends, waiting for an opening at the launch site. Not far downriver, Big Bill has another hit, this one yanking his rod down and snapping his line.

He starts to hurl his new rod and reel overboard. "Wait," I scream, "don't blame the fishing pole. It may have been a seal."

"Say, what?"

"You heard me. Maybe you hooked into a seal. I read about one visiting this area all summer."

"You've been on the river too long," he says.

I was joking that a seal would bite his creepy crawler, but was dead serious about the seal cruising the river. Actually, the seal was seen downstream a couple miles, below the Holyoke Dam, where marine biologists said these sightings were perhaps the farthest inland seal sightings on the river (South Hadley is about 100 miles from the river's mouth). The one-hundred-pound seal was probably a harbor seal, which occasionally come upriver but rarely to Hartford, let alone into Massachusetts.

We drift downriver, admiring our first view of Mount Tom poking up through the clouds. In some spots the shoreline has a steep ledge of rock, and one house on a point of land has a commanding upriver view. We see someone inside sitting at the kitchen table enjoying a cup of coffee or tea, perhaps wondering what possesses Big Bill and me to be out on the river on such a miserable day. But we're having a ball, teasing and arguing like we did in high school, and laughing while the rain drips off Big Bill's snazzy Orvis hat and into his lap.

The river is narrow here and has a bit of a chop. I shut the motor, lift the propeller out of the water, insert the oars, and start rowing toward the west bank.

"What are you doing?" Big Bill asks.

"Trust me," I say.

Beneath us, in relatively shallow water, are a series of ledges that would have ripped the propeller from the engine. I paddle to the gently sloping ledge on the shoreline and beach the boat.

"Let's go," I say. "It's only a short walk."

Big Bill follows and we walk the shoreline, heading up the bank a short way.

I point down to the shale. "Aren't these great? See the three toes?"

The tracks are from a dinosaur, made about 190 million years ago in the late Triassic and early Jurassic periods. The fifteen-inch tracks, part of a small, eight-acre property called Dinosaur Tracks Reservation owned by The Trustees of Reservations, are referred to as Eubrontes tracks and are said to have been made by upright walking, meat-eating dinosaurs approximately twenty feet in length. All the tracks have three toes and are birdlike, as if a two-story-tall great blue heron had been hunting here. Several tracks are quite distinct, set down an inch into the rock, and I take several pictures. It's one thing to see *Jurassic Park* at the movies, but quite another to stand in the very spot where the great creatures once lived.

Although these tracks and the ones in Rocky Hill, Connecticut, are the most visible, the Connecticut River valley has thousands of dinosaur tracks. The first tracks recorded in New England were found in 1802 on the opposite side of the river in South Hadley, when Pliny Moody was plowing his fields. He said Noah's raven made them because they resembled the tracks of a bird.

The tracks make me think about humankind's arrival in New England, a mere 13,000 years ago when the Paleo tribe arrived. Retreating glaciers left behind a cold, barren landscape where woolly mammoths, mastodon, and caribou roamed. Paleos followed in family-sized bands, hunting with spears sometimes thrown using an *atlatl* or throwing stick.

The spear points used by prehistoric people for hunting and butchering animals are of a distinctive shape, with a flute or channel on each side called fluted points. A significant number of artifacts have been found in only a handful of Paleo sites in New England. Bull Brook in Ipswich is the largest Paleo site in New England, but a smaller site was found along the Connecticut River near Sugarloaf.

I have a special interest in the period because my late brother-in-law, Fred Carty, and his uncle, Stanley Buzarewicz, uncovered a Paleo site along the Neponset River in Eastern Massachusetts, now on exhibit at the Peabody Museum in Andover, Massachusetts. To hold one of the carefully crafted fluted points is a thrill in itself; another human, thousands of years earlier, held the same point and depended upon it for his or her life. Even better was the *atlatl* Stanley made for me. We took it to a football field along with a spear. Using the *atlatl*, I was able to hurl the spear the length of the field with such accuracy it almost hit the goalpost.

From the making of the dinosaur tracks before me to the making of rhyolite fluted points, millions of years had passed. Sure makes you think about how insignificant our time is on earth, a message not to take life too seriously.

We push the boat back into the river and drift along the edge of the shore, occasionally using the oar to keep us parallel with the fallen trees and in casting position. Big Bill catches one more smallmouth, this one a three-pounder, and the city slicker with the $10 rod and reel has completely outfished me. When we see the string of barrels stretched across the river to alert us to the danger of the Holyoke Dam, we fire up the motor and head home. The rain comes down in sheets but we still have smiles, knowing the river gave two old friends a day to remember.

12

Holyoke, Massachusetts, to the Connecticut Border

Perhaps more than any other city, Holyoke's boom years were directly related to the river. Here the power of the Connecticut could be easily harnessed because of the river's sixty-foot drop within a fifth of a mile at South Hadley Falls. Holyoke's first dam spanning the full width of the river was constructed in 1848 out of hemlock timbers and was thought to be the largest one in the world. Incredibly, on the dam's initial day of operation it failed miserably—giving way within four hours of the closing of its gates. A telegraph to Boston reported that within two hours of the gates' closing the dam was "leaking badly;" at four hours the telegraph read "stones of bulkhead giving way to pressure;" and by 3:20 P.M. the smart aleck operating the telegraph machine hammered out "Your old dam's gone to hell by way of Willimansett."

But the city went back at it and within a year a new dam was erected along with not one, but three interconnected canals. The concept was to use the same river water three times. Walter Hard, in *The Connecticut*, describes the design as follows: "First the water entered the upper canal. There was a row of mills and raceways between it and a parallel canal, on a lower level, that received the water that had poured through the mill wheels. This water powered the mills on the second level, and passed to the third canal."

An entire manufacturing community was planned around the construction of the canals, making Holyoke one of the first planned industrial communities in the nation. A group of business investors, primarily from Boston and Hartford, bought twelve hundred acres of land along the river and began erecting roads for stores and boarding houses for the mill workers. The investors lost their shirts on the scheme. Maybe they were ahead of their time or maybe they were simply overambitious, but the numerous mills erected were not needed at the time.

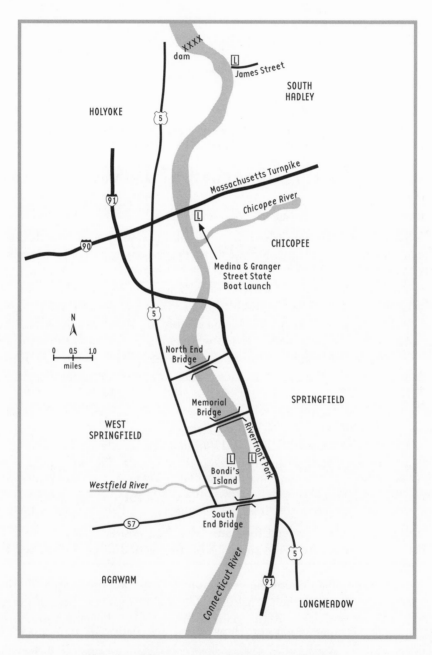

HOLYOKE, MASS., TO THE CONNECTICUT BORDER

New management eventually took over the industrial community and a variety of mills were successful, producing goods from textiles to machinery. However, Holyoke will always be known for its paper mills — more writing paper and envelopes were manufactured here than anywhere else in the United States. Today mills are still in operation, but business is more diversified.

❖　❖　❖

As a kid I fished the Holyoke Dam. (The present day dam is the third one at the spot and is comprised mostly of granite.) Shoulder-to-shoulder with other anglers, we cast out shad darts and, with no particular skill, invariably caught a shad or two.

Prime-time shad fishing is during May and early June, when the fish congregate in the rapids below the dam. Relatively clear water ranging in temperature from sixty to sixty-five degrees provides optimum conditions for shad to strike. (Sometimes there are so many fish they can even be seen while standing on the Route 116 bridge. For a close-up look visit the viewing station at the South Hadley Falls fish ladder.)

A shad dart, which is a hook with a colorful weight around it, can be quite effective, probably angering the shad into striking. They also can be taken on a fly rod, using a shad fly on extra fast sinking line. Whether spin casting or fly-fishing, anglers should cast across the river and keep a tight line, so the fly or lure will drag near the bottom as you work it back to shore. (The mouths of shad are small, so you will want a small hook such as a size four or six.) Though referred to as a poor man's salmon, a big shad is a thrill to hook; catching several in an hour is a ball. (This is why you won't be the only angler fishing below the South Hadley Falls Bridge.)

Like the salmon, shad are an anadromous fish, living in salt water and traveling upstream to spawn in fresh water. Once they spawn, leaving behind billions of eggs, the adults will return to the sea. The newly hatched shad will grow in the river or a tributary. Those that survive attacks from predators, including birds and bigger fish, will swim to the ocean in the fall. In the ocean, they will feed and grow for two to five years, some to a weight of five or six pounds, before returning to the river to spawn as adults.

❖　❖　❖

If the fishing is so much fun, how about the paddling? Not good. I paddled a portion of the stretch between Holyoke and the Connecticut border once, and the river was not conducive to canoeing or kayaking.

Antiquated sewer systems still discharge untreated sewage into the river during periods of heavy rain. Still, the river is far cleaner today than it was thirty years ago when rafts of sludge bobbed on the surface. And today the river won't surprise you by its color, as in the days of the woolen mills when dyes of every imaginable hue stained the current differently each day.

For me, the real problem is the almost continuous development along the riverbanks, making it all but impossible to connect with nature. Factories, old mills, warehouses, high-tension power lines, and sewage treatment plants dot the shoreline through Holyoke, Chicopee, Springfield, and West Springfield. Not everyone, however, feels this way. Several of my friends love the river here, pointing out that if you're in something bigger than a canoe, a day on the water can be quite relaxing.

The city of Springfield reflects the morning sun.

If you do take a paddle or a boat ride from Holyoke to the Connecticut border (about eighteen miles), you could begin at the Department of Environmental Management launch site on Canal Street in South Hadley, about a quarter-mile below the Route 116 bridge. (Near the launch site the river can be shallow in the summer and swift most anytime.) The river flows for about five or six miles, passing bridges, dikes, and a private marina until the next public launch at Chicopee (off Medina and Granger

Streets, just below where the Massachusetts Turnpike crosses the Connecticut.)

Next, the Chicopee River, the Connecticut River's largest tributary, enters from the east, draining 720 square miles. Four more miles down-river, Springfield is on the east and West Springfield on the west, connected by the North End Bridge. A mile and a half more and you come to the handsome Memorial Bridge with its seven granite spires and globe-shaped caps. If the bridge looks vaguely familiar to people who have never been in Springfield before, it's probably because it was featured promi-nently in a movie from the 1970s titled *The Reincarnation of Peter Proud*.

Springfield has a small riverfront park, and visitors can enjoy a day-time or twilight cruise on the *Tinkerbell* Peter Pan River Bus, which departs from the park. (It's too bad most of Springfield is blocked from the river by Interstate 91. The Basketball Hall of Fame is one of the few tourist destinations located close to the water.) A mile farther downstream on the West Springfield side of the river is a public boat launch just off Route 5 at Bondi's Island. (Bondi's Island is primarily the site of a regional wastewater treatment plant.) On the opposite bank the Mill River, which drains Watershops Pond, enters the Connecticut. In another half-mile is the confluence of the Westfield River, followed by the South End Bridge and Springfield Yacht Club. The town of Agawam and Six Flags Amusement Park are now on the west bank, and Longmeadow is on the east. This is the widest point on the river at 2,100 feet.

Boating is relatively peaceful and quiet here, as the shoreline is wooded once again and Interstate 91 no longer runs within sight of the river. Before you reach the hiking trails at Fanny Stebbins Wildlife Sanctuary in Longmeadow, you will come to the Pioneer Valley Yacht Club, also in Longmeadow. Tiny Willy's Island is one mile before the Connecticut border, and it's three miles to Enfield Dam.

Don't be surprised to see some shallow spots as you float through Greater Springfield; the river is lower today than it was several years ago. There are differing opinions as to the cause. Some say that the lower water is partially due to the crumbling of the Enfield Dam. The cause, however, is probably more complex, and the question remains as to whether restoring the dam would affect the water levels.

❖   ❖   ❖

Before the Europeans arrived in Springfield, Native Americans lived quite comfortably here, using the Connecticut, the Chicopee, and the Westfield Rivers as travel routes and sources of food, akin to our highways and supermarkets. The lowlands with rich soil were used as planting grounds, and the high bluff at modern day Long Hill (near the Longmeadow border) was perfect for a defensive fort. The native's downfall, it could be argued, began on a spring day in 1636, when they allowed William Pynchon and his followers to erect square houses. Pynchon had great success trading with the natives as evidenced by the quantity of pelts—2,620 in 1654—he shipped downriver from Springfield. His business was so prosperous he even built a warehouse on the east bank at the Enfield Rapids; pelts could be transferred from canoe to the warehouse to await larger ships coming up the river. (The area is still known as Warehouse Point.)

For years the Native Americans and the newcomers coexisted, and archeological digs at the Long Hill site confirm this indeed was a contact site: the natives were combining their way of life with changes introduced by the settlers. Besides the traditional stone points, copper points; three-pronged iron fish spears; Dutch fairy pipes from Bristol, England; an iron pot; and an unusual Indian pottery cup in a form resembling an English mug were all found here.

When King Philip's War broke out in June of 1675, the natives around Springfield initially remained peaceful. But as the war spread westward and upriver towns were destroyed, it was clear that Springfield was next in the line of fire. John Pynchon, the son of the founding father, was in control at the time. On October 4 he led a large body of Springfield militia to join with troops at Hadley for a strike to the north. Of course, this left Springfield virtually defenseless, a fact which was not lost on the increasingly hostile Agawams.

In *King Philip's War*, co-author Eric Schultz writes that "on the night of October 4 as many as several hundred additional warriors had been secretly admitted into the Agawam village. With their encouragement, a plan was devised to attack Springfield the following morning, once Pynchon's troops were well clear of the town. This plot was revealed by Toto, an Indian employed by an English family at Windsor, Connecticut. Messengers were sent to Springfield on October 5 and managed to awaken residents and gather the population in three fortified houses. A messenger was sent to Hadley to recall the recently departed troops.

"When all remained quiet on the morning of October 5, Lieutenant Cooper and Thomas Miller, the town's constable, decided to ride to Fort Hill and investigate. Cooper in particular was convinced that the Agawam would remain loyal to the English despite hostilities throughout the valley. He was wrong: only a short distance from the garrisons the two were ambushed. Miller died instantly but Cooper kept his mount long enough to warn the nearest garrison, at which point he also died."

The warriors then attacked the garrisons and set the unoccupied buildings ablaze, burning thirty-two houses and twenty-five barns. The people in the garrisons would have all been killed had not Major Robert Treat arrived from Connecticut on the west bank of the Connecticut River. Although he was unable to cross due to enemy fire, he managed to occupy the natives long enough for Major Pynchon to arrive. The native forces withdrew to Indian Orchard near the Chicopee River and only thirteen houses were left standing in the center of Springfield.

Springfield was not attacked again, but, on March 26, 1676, a band of settlers were ambushed while walking to church from Longmeadow to Springfield. Two settlers were killed and captured. At the time most of the early settlers of Longmeadow lived down by the river rather than near the present-day common. An old map of Longmeadow land grants shows rectangular parcels of land along the river, which allowed each owner direct access to the Connecticut. These lots, however, are in an area of frequent flooding, so it's no wonder the original grants have reverted back to woods and future settlement was done on higher ground.

The west side of the river, in present day Agawam, was used primarily for grazing of horse and cattle owned by the Springfield settlers. The animals fed in the rich natural meadows along the river from spring until November, and the district became known as Feeding Hills.

Springfield survived the Native American raids and went on to prosper, particularly as a manufacturing center of arms. George Washington selected Springfield as the site for one of two U.S. armory and arsenals, and every type of firearm was made here from muskets to the famous Springfield rifle. (A portion of the Springfield Armory was established as a national historic site.)

❖   ❖   ❖

Although I don't recommend taking a canoe or kayak through Greater Springfield, this stretch of river is still close to my heart. My favorite place both in my childhood and now is the 800 acres of fields and woodlands known as the Meadows, land owned by Longmeadow Conservation Commission and the Fanny Stebbins Wildlife Sanctuary.

The floodplain at the meadows is a superb birding spot, where one can see great blue herons, green-backed herons, and kingfishers all hunting for fish in the ponds and streams near the river. Coyotes, deer, and beaver also live here. In some places the flooding water of the river has whisked away most undergrowth, leaving only a few giant maples and cottonwoods behind and giving the shoreline a parklike look.

13

ENFIELD, CONNECTICUT, TO WETHERSFIELD, CONNECTICUT

The power of the river eventually overcomes most human handiwork, and crumbling Enfield Dam is a good example. At one time the rock-and-timber dam was nine feet tall and built to channel river flow into the Windsor Locks canal, but the ceaseless current has knocked over most of it. There are no plans to rebuild the dam and the river will return to its natural state. The remains of the dam, however, are clearly visible, crossing the river in a diagonal line; paddlers should not run these tricky rapids. Perhaps in low water a paddler could do a little scouting and half float, half drag a vessel through the riprap, but I wouldn't try it. If you stand on the Suffield side of the dam, you can see water funneling through rocky debris into churning chutes where it curls back on itself. Hydraulics like these have sucked more than one boater to a deadly fate. Even if you make it over the remains of the dam, considerable rapids and obstructions await you downstream.

Motorboats should be particularly careful here. Above the rapids is the Donald Barnes Boat Launch on Asnuntuck Street in Enfield. I meet a boater there who tells me a tale of woe from last spring. "We thought we went through the rapids with no problem during high water. But we had actually hit bottom and the sheer pin on the propeller broke. The current was so fast we didn't notice the propeller wasn't turning, until we tried to go back. Then we realized the problem but we were four miles from the launch site. Believe it or not we actually got out, and with one guy pulling and two pushing, we slogged through water all the way back to the launch. At least we made it safely—the current is strong, even above the dam, and there have been drownings here."

As for fishing, "It can be mobbed in the spring with fishermen. They used to be after the shad, but now most of them come for the striped bass. A few forty-inchers have been caught here. And there's plenty of boats here, too. I've even seen some go right up the rapids and over the old dam in high water."

Stripers are beautiful silver fish, which come up from Long Island Sound to forage on the alewives and shad migrating upstream. It might be crowded in the spring, but it is worth the trip to have the outside shot at catching a striper.

The famous Windsor Locks and Enfield Canal begin here at the dam, where water from the river is diverted under a stone and cement bridge and into the canal. Although boats no longer use the canal, it allowed vessels to bypass the six-mile Enfield Rapids and eliminate poling, towing, or portaging. The arrival of the railroads coincided with completion of the canal and business on the canal slowed. The canal stayed viable by generating power for the growing number of mills and factories along its banks.

As water commerce was crucial in the 1800s, business owners in New Haven wanted to siphon off some of the Connecticut River trade. In a loan report seeking funds for the canal, the New Haven business community pointed out that "having no river flowing into our waters and cut off from the places above us, and around us, unless we can unite ourselves with those places by artificial means, our business must remain local in character and limited in extent." Work on the Farmington Canal began in 1825 and it reached Farmington in 1828 and Northampton in 1835. This colossal canal was not without its problems. Aqueducts, sixty locks, and embankments had to be maintained, and drought and flood slowed traffic. After all the work and investment needed to build the canal, it ceased operation just a short time later in 1847, when the faster and more efficient railroads made it obsolete.

The Enfield Canal was built to keep boat traffic coming up the river through Hartford rather than bypassing the city altogether on the Farmington Canal. Shorter and more effective, the Enfield Canal had boats lined up to use it when it opened in 1829. In *Abandoned New England* author William F. Robinson writes that the canal "was successful, and the town of Windsor Locks that sprang up at its southern end became a favorite haunt of rivermen as it mushroomed into the gamblingest, drunkenest, bawdiest town in New England."

The old towpath on the canal now serves for walking and bicycling, running for 4.5 miles between the canal on one side and the river on the other. It begins at the Enfield Dam parking lot on Canal Street in Suffield and follows the river south, passing King's Island and ending near Route 140. When you walk the towpath, consider that the eighty-foot-wide canal was dug by the backbreaking labor of Irishmen imported for the job, many of whom did not live to return to their homeland. (The bike path is closed from November 14 through April 1 because of the bald eagles that winter here. The river stays free of ice in the rapids and the birds are able

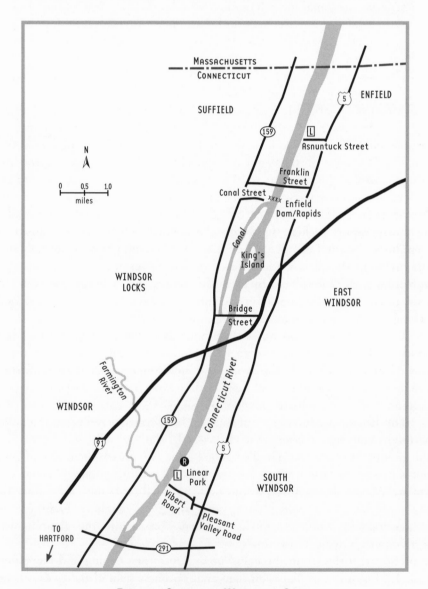

ENFIELD, CONN., TO WINDSOR, CONN.

Although boats no longer use the Windsor Locks and Enfield Canal, it was quite useful in its day, allowing vessels to bypass the six-mile Enfield Rapids.

to catch fish. Downstream from the rapids by King's Island is the northernmost spot where the effects of the tide reach.)

The most interesting spot on the towpath/bike trail is in Suffield, where Stony Brook is located. The brook passes beneath the canal on a new aqueduct, which is adjacent to the original stone aqueduct. The old aqueduct is New England's last complete stone aqueduct still standing, and is sixty feet wide and 104 feet long.

The northern section of the canal is in a wooded setting, but farther south, at Windsor Locks, it's closer to the road and industrial buildings. It runs parallel to South Main Street and factories separate the canal from the river. Unfortunately, paddling and boating anywhere on the canal is prohibited. The Dexter Corporation owns the canal and made this decision because of liability concerns—several low bridges span the canal and there's no easy access to the river.

Below Windsor Locks is the historic town of Windsor, where the Farmington River meets the Connecticut. A nice park sits along the Farmington at Route 159 as well as several historic homes, including the Walter Fyler House, which dates back to 1640. Windsor calls itself "the first permanent settlement in Connecticut." The events leading up to this settlement are a little confusing, but they begin with the first European exploration of the Connecticut River by Dutch sea captain Adrian Block in 1614. In his sloop the *Onrust* (meaning restless) Block ventured upriver to the modern day town of South Windsor, where the Podunk tribe told him of the many furbearing animals in the region. Thinking of going farther into the interior of the New World, he continued up the river, but the Enfield Rapids turned him back. He returned to Europe, spreading the word of the fur trade. It wasn't until 1633 that the Dutch built a fort up the river, erecting the House of Good Hope, a trading post at what is now Hartford.

The Pilgrims also had their eye on the area, ever since Edward Winslow sailed up the river in 1632. Winslow was invited to settle on the river by the Podunks, who hoped Pilgrim muskets would help defend them against the more powerful Pequots. The Pilgrims took the Podunks up on the offer, wanting to get the upper hand in the fur trade. In 1633 William Holmes of Plymouth Colony sailed to the present day site of Windsor, where he erected a frame house he brought with him on his sloop.

The Puritans sent John Oldham on an overland route from Massachusetts Bay Colony to establish a settlement at Wethersfield. Although Oldham's followers barely survived the first winter (it was so cold the river was frozen solid by November 15), more Puritans followed in 1636; most notably Reverend Thomas Hooker who settled his group at Hartford near the Dutch fort, and William Pynchon who pushed on to Agawam and later Springfield.

While the Podunk tribe welcomed all the newcomers, the Pequots did not, probably feeling vulnerable on their western flank as the number of Dutch and English climbed. Initially, the Pequots were involved in two coastal fights against individual Englishmen, including the killing of John Oldham off Block Island. Massachusetts Bay Colony responded by dispatching a group of soldiers under the leadership of Captain John Endecott, to take revenge. Endecott succeeded in killing a few Pequots and burning their provisions before he made a hasty withdrawal back to Boston, leaving enraged Pequots behind. The natives soon attacked Wethersfield. Windsor increased its fortifications, digging a wide ditch and inner earth rampart that was embedded with tree trunks. Called the Palisado, the fortification encircled the inner part of the town.

The European settlements along the river then united, raising a force of ninety settlers under Captain John Mason. On the morning of May 26, 1637, they attacked the Pequots while they slept in their Mystic Fort. Mason surrounded the fort, poured in volley after volley of musket balls, then torched the wigwams, burning women and children along with the male warriors. The slaughter of the Pequots was particularly gruesome, as evidenced by the research of writer Neil Asher Silberman: "As the fire quickly spread among the closely packed wigwams, Mason ordered his men to retreat. Once outside the wall, determined not to leave the work unfinished, he arrayed his troops in a tight ring around the burning village to prevent the escape of any of its inhabitants. While some tried desperately to climb over the high stockade wall, others resigned themselves to the flames." Even the Mohegans and Narragansetts who fought with Mason were horrified by the Englishman's method of war, telling Mason "it is too furious and slays too many men." The Reverend Cotton Mather, however, mixed the fearful sight with religious overtones of righteousness: "to see them thus frying in ye fyer, and ye streams of blood quenching ye same, and horrible was ye stinck and sente thereof: but ye victory seemed a sweet sacrafice, and they gave prayse thereof to God." Most of the surviving Pequots were hunted down and the war was over within a matter of weeks.

Not long after the Pequot War, Windsor grew to the point a ferry was established. A sign on Route 159 reads: "This marks the road to Bissell's Ferry, established by the General Court of Connecticut in 1641, operated by the Bissell Family for nearly 100 years, later leased to various towns-men and continually operated until 1917." At the end of the dirt road adjacent to the sign is the site of the ferry on the banks of the river beneath some towering cottonwoods.

❖   ❖   ❖

For paddling through Greater Hartford, I decide to launch about ten miles below the Enfield Dam at the South Windsor Boat Launch at Linear Park, located on Vibert Road. It's a balmy November day and most river-lovers have put their boats away for the year. I wonder about the warming of the planet when I realize this was the month the river froze solid in the early 1600s when Oldham arrived. And here I am in shirtsleeves with temperatures in the upper sixties.

Once in the river I realize I'm far enough downstream from the dam to avoid treacherous currents, but there are plenty of sandbars and shallows. I could paddle upstream and poke into the mouth of the Farmington River, which is hidden by an island, but instead I go with the current to make the day easier. I'm in my kayak, so there's no electric motor to fall back on.

Passing beneath the Route 291 overpass, I paddle over to the Bissell Bridge Boat Launch and meet a professor and a group of students from West Hartford's Saint Joseph College. They are testing the water and tell me it is a bit high in phosphate, probably from sewer overflow. However, the professor says, based on fifteen years of testing and the health of the fish, the river is slowly getting cleaner. The problem, he explains, is after rainstorms when phosphates from sewage get flushed into the river, resulting in increased algae growth.

Most of the shoreline I paddle by is wooded, but I know beyond the trees are a few remaining tobacco fields. Tobacco thrives in the valley's dry porous soil and humid climate by the river. The cured tobacco leaves grown here make some of the world's finest cigar wrappers. Tobacco was the main crop of the river valley in the nineteenth century, but faltered when a superior product was exported from Sumatra where it's usually hot with overcast skies. Connecticut River farmers were ingenious,

I continue downriver, noticing how handsome a city skyline can look from the water.

if nothing else, and began erecting gauzelike netting above their plants to duplicate the shade of Sumatra. Today development has pushed out most of the farms, but in towns like Suffield and Windsor, motorists can still see acres of flimsy cheesecloth shading tobacco plants.

A couple of miles below the Bissell Boat Launch I paddle beneath a railroad bridge to see my first boat of the morning as I enter the city limits of Hartford. On the west bank is Riverside Park with its large parking area and boat launch. In the warm weather months it is jammed with boat trailers, but today just a few cars are in the lot. I pull over and stretch my legs.

The park is an impressive use of urban land, complete with tree-lined pathways, playground, and picnic area. I strike up a conversation with a young man who has just finished backing his trailered bass boat into the river. "It was real shallow here this summer," he said. "See those gulls out in the river? They're standing on a sandbar. All that was exposed a couple months ago."

"How's the fishing?" I ask.

"Actually, pretty good, considering we're in Hartford," he says. "We catch largemouth bass and northern pike downriver, and when the water's high enough to go upstream we sometimes get smallmouths."

I tell him I'm writing a book about the river, and how I was apprehensive about coming through this urban section. "Well," he laughed, "you picked the right day. Not many people expected a Sunday in November to be perfect boating weather. In the summer I try to get here at the crack of dawn and be off the river in three or four hours before all the day-boaters come." Before we leave he hands me his card and says to call him in the spring if I want to join him for a day of fishing on the river.

I push off and continue downriver, noticing how handsome a city skyline can look from the water. Hartford seems to be doing a good job reclaiming its riverfront. The riverside parks are part of a major revitalization effort that has been underway for twenty years by Riverfront Recapture, a public-private partnership that has won national awards for creating a system of parks and trails. A lighted bicycle path curves along the west bank, heading downriver from Riverfront Park toward Adiaen's Landing. Along the way the path passes a small park of terraced levels of rust-colored stone and concrete rising from the river. Just downriver is another unique landmark, the blue, onion-shaped dome of the Colt Armory. Samuel Colt, the inventor of the Colt six-shooter, built the armory in 1854, and protected it from river flooding by building aseries of dikes. Colt first patented the repeating revolver in 1836. Its success was due to replaceable parts, which allowed weapons to be repaired even after they were damaged on the battlefield. Perhaps because of the Colt Factory's close proximity to the Federal Armory in Springfield, Colt had many government contracts during the Civil War and afterward. The Connecticut River valley became known for its production of firearms, a foreshadowing of Connecticut's prominence in the defense industry.

On the east bank of the river in East Hartford is Great River Park and Boat Launch. I meet a couple out walking their dog. We agree we are fortunate that some of the riverfront was kept as open space. To be sure, plenty of industry abuts the river here, such as the large brick power plant on the west side, but the pedestrian walkways are a step in the right direction. The walkers also tell me to be careful because huge barges

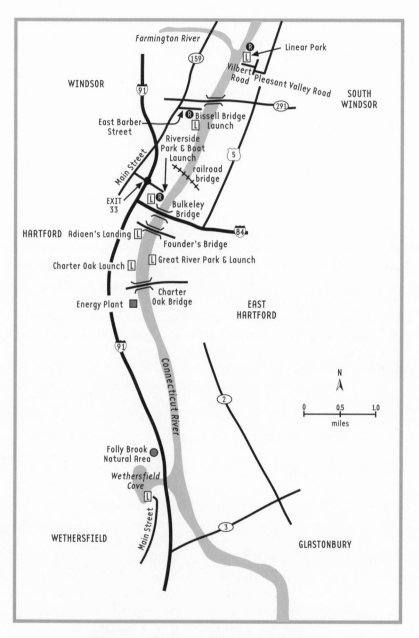

WINDSOR, CONN., TO WETHERSFIELD, CONN.

come up the river. (Barges and tugs can reach Hartford because this is the northernmost section of a channel that is regularly dredged by the Army Corps of Engineers.)

Once I pass the Charter Oak Bridge it's a relatively uneventful two-mile paddle to the narrow passage into Wethersfield Cove. I'm a little ahead of schedule and my ride has yet to arrive, so I walk over to the Cove Warehouse, now a seasonal museum. The warehouse dates back to 1690 and was built when the river's path was much closer to the cove. It's evident the cove was also broader because the doors to the warehouse are at a considerable height above the current water level. Wethersfield argues with Windsor that it is the oldest town in Connecticut, but no matter: both are beautiful and have a full share of history. The *Tryall*, the first ship built on the river, was erected here in Wethersfield in 1649, and shipbuilding was an important part of the town's early growth. Several warehouses were built to store corn, onion, beaver skins, brick, and fish to be shipped downriver.

I sit in the sun by the Cove Warehouse, munching an apple and thinking of all the people from times gone by that probably sat in the same place. Then I hear a horn toot and my ride is here. With a little luck I'll be back in the spring for the final leg of my river days.

14

WETHERSFIELD, CONNECTICUT, TO EAST HADDAM, CONNECTICUT

The Glastonbury/Rocky Hill Ferry has been running since 1655 and is the nation's oldest continually operating ferry. Like the warehouse at Wethersfield Cove, it carries a river-lover back to a simpler time when the pace in the valley was much slower. Ferrymen first used poles and oars to cross the river and soon graduated to horsepower, placing the horse on a treadmill. Today, with the aid of a little bright red and black tugboat, the ferry will transport you across the river in a relaxing five-minute ride.

Of course, 1655 may seem like a long time a go, but Rocky Hill is steeped in a history that encompasses dinosaurs and glacial lakes. Rocky Hill was the southern terminus of Lake Hitchcock, thought to have developed 13,700 years ago when sediment from melting glaciers created a dam, trapping the water and extending it back all the way to Lyme, New Hampshire. The 150-mile-long lake was thought to be eight miles wide in spots. When the dam collapsed, perhaps 10,000 years ago, the lake drained to the ocean, leaving behind the fertile farmland. Geologists point out that when the dam gave way, such a tremendous amount of water poured out that evidence of this scouring still exists at the top of the lofty ridge where Gillette Castle stands downriver in East Haddam.

Long before the glaciers came the dinosaurs. While the tracks in South Hadley and Holyoke were discovered in the 1800s, the tracks at Rocky Hill were not unearthed until 1966. But what a find; the park is the largest dinosaur track site in North America. The dinosaur footprints are exhibited exactly where they were found, but now a huge geodesic dome keeps the tracks safe and the viewer indoors. The hundreds of prints from three-toed meat eaters made when the climate of Connecticut was subtropical are approximately 185 million years old. Although it would seem that these tracks are from a large congregation of dinosaurs, they were made at different time periods.

The Glastonbury/Rocky Hill Ferry has been running since 1655 and is the nation's oldest, continually operating ferry.

Referred to as Eubrontes tracks, the maker of the tracks resembled Dilophosaurus, a twenty-foot-long birdlike carnivore that walked upright on powerful hind legs. The tracks were made in soft, sandy mud and then preserved when other sediments washed over them. The area was then compressed by additional sediments and turned into sandstone. (A circular walkway had been constructed around the tracks and a sound system pipes in the dinosaurs' roars and sounds of a tropical jungle.)

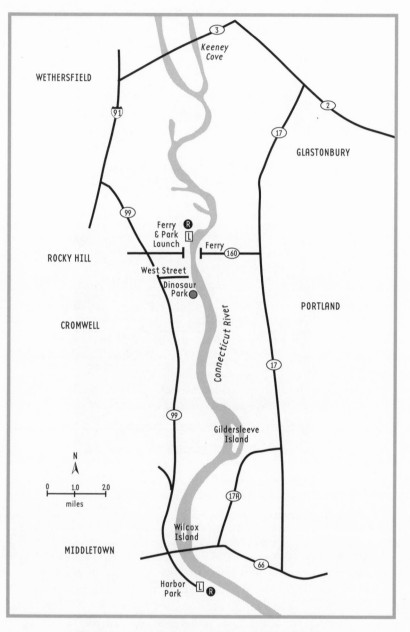

WETHERSFIELD, CONN., TO MIDDLETOWN, CONN.

❖ ❖ ❖

At 8:00 A.M. on a weekday I meet Al Allgeier at the Rocky Hill Boat Launch for a cruise downriver in his boat. I met Al the prior autumn when I paddled through Hartford; he warned me the river could be terribly crowded with big boats on weekends. When I explained I'd canoed or kayaked most of the river from the source, he offered to give me a tour of the river from the comfort of his boat. I jumped at the chance, deciding I could see the main stem of the river with Al, then kayak the coves, estuaries, and passages around the islands on my own. Al has been going up and down the river for the last ten years; doing sections of the river, but never boating from Wethersfield to the ocean in a day trip as we have planned for today.

From Rocky Hill the river flows relatively straight with very little development along its banks, except for an occasional home set high up on a ridge. About five miles down when we enter Cromwell, Gildersleeve Island splits the river and the deeper channel has formed toward the east bank. (Paddlers should try the shallower west side passage as it will have fewer big boats. Look out for the submerged dike across this passage, which channels water to the eastern side for larger boats.) The island is totally wooded and Al tells me that on weekends boaters picnic on the sandy beach opposite the southern end of the island on the west side of the river.

The river stretches out before us, carving its way through green hills, and small clouds, like white cotton balls, dot the deep blue sky. I comment to Al how fresh the river smells and how surprised I am to be cruising through an area of lush forest rather than homes. "That's why I love being out on the boat," says Al. "It's just me and the river. I feel like I'm driving right through a picture."

Another island, Wilcox Island, is located above Middletown. Evidence of the town's shipping past can be seen in the granite walls built along the banks to allow schooners to pull up to the shore. (During the Revolution, the Gildersleeve shipyard in Portland produced the 700-ton *Trumbull*.) Above the Arrigoni bridge, which connects Portland to Middletown, the surroundings abruptly change from countryside to commercial as the two towns crowd the river. About a mile farther on the west bank are Harbor Park and the America's Cup Restaurant, where boaters can moor at the dock and dine in the restaurant.

If you look at a map of Connecticut you will notice the river is flowing due south all the way to Middletown, then abruptly turns to the southeast due to the metamorphic rock in the surrounding ridges. Steep walls of ledge plunge down to the river, making this section far different from the broad floodplains of the Greater Hartford area and the Pioneer Valley.

Boaters start to feel the effects of the tide near Middletown, though the water is still fresh. The river itself changes as well, becoming deeper as it carves through hilly country. The shoreline below Middletown becomes mostly wooded again, except for a power plant and tanker dock that mar the natural scenery. Dart Island is located about four miles below the Arrigoni bridge, and two miles beyond on the east bank is one of the river's better state parks. Hurd Park has a wonderful river trail winding through large oak, ash, maple, and hemlock before bringing you to the banks of the Connecticut and a grassy opening with picnic benches. It's a nice place to sit and watch the boats, big and small, cruising the river.

The hemlock at Hurd Park are suffering from the effects of hemlock woolly adelgid, a minuscule bug that sucks the tree's sap and leaves a toxic saliva. Damage to the hemlock is severe. When a tree is attacked it takes four or five years until it dies—first the crown thins followed by yellowed needles. Some trees survive, usually those on cooler, moister north- and east-facing slopes. To date the best hope to combat the adelgid is one of their natural predators, a ladybug introduced here from Japan.

South of Hurd Park is Haddam Island, with a nice sandy beach for picnicking, and Haddam Meadows State Park with its launch site on the western side of the river. On the opposite shoreline is Connecticut Yankee Atomic Power Plant. Al says the Haddam Meadows launch is one of the better ones on the river, but even though it's far from the population center of Hartford, he still avoids it on weekends. In fact, he will only come on the river during the week because of boat traffic on the week-ends. "You're always rocking in somebody else's wake, and the big boats have no mercy on the little ones. You need to pay attention because there are long sandbars in the river, like the one just a couple hundred feet down from here."

Al recalls that not all of his trips are good ones and it's not just because of too many people or sandbars. "A couple years ago I was boating here when out of nowhere a thunderstorm hit. It was only fifteen minutes long, but I was scared to death. Lightning was literally hitting the water then bouncing off. Rain was so hard it hurt the skin. I just crouched down and prayed."

After we pass the mouth of the Salmon River we begin to see more impressive riverfront homes. We pass one relatively modest home I'd be quite happy with. It seems to be built right into the hillside, almost at water level, and has porches on both its second and third floors overlooking the river. It must be wonderful to sit on the upper deck and watch the river go by in all seasons.

A mile below the Salmon River is the turnstile bridge connecting Haddam with East Haddam. Built in 1913 it is one of the largest swing bridges in the country, and barges and tugs can pass on either side of the center support. (In 1986 the bridge was overhauled, but the changes made may have caused more harm than good. The bridge's steel grid deck was paved over, which may have made it too heavy for its gears and bearings, causing several malfunctions.) In the shadow of the bridge on the west bank, the fleet of Camelot Cruise Ships lies anchored at Marine Park. Dinner cruises are offered, as well as a cruise down the Connecticut River and across Long Island Sound, docking at Sag Harbor or Greenport before the return.

The Goodspeed Opera House rises on the east bank of the bridge. This white Victorian, built just after the Civil War, graces the river with its beauty. When the ornate six-story opera house first opened, it included a freight and passenger station for the New York Steamboat Company. The opera house gave birth to *Annie*, *Man of La Mancha*, and *Shenandoah*. In 1952 it was slated to be torn down, but concerned citizens bought it for a dollar. A million-dollar restoration followed and Goodspeed was back in business in 1963; it is still the tallest all-wooden structure on the Connecticut.

East Haddam is full of history, some of it obscure but fascinating, like the story of Venture Smith, a man from Guinea who was sold into slavery and brought to Haddam by a sea captain. Over time he was able to earn enough money to buy his freedom. Legend has it he was so strong he could carry a barrel of molasses on each shoulder, and once cut four hundred cords of wood in a few weeks. He also dictated his autobiography, which was popular enough to go through several printings. His gravestone in the East Haddam Cemetery reads: "Sacred to the memory of Venture Smith, African, though the son of a king he was kidnapped and sold as a slave, but by his industry, he acquired money to purchase his freedom, who died Sept 19th in ye 77th year of his age."

Also below the opera house are Rich and Lord Islands, which lie side by side and create two narrow channels around them. Paddlers and anglers should investigate these shallow passages and look for one of two small creeks on the east bank that lead into Chapman Pond. This area is known for great largemouth and northern pike fishing along the weed bed that surrounds the entire pond. (Both creeks have obstructions making navigation difficult.)

Rivaling the opera house with its splendor is Gillette Castle, perched on a ridge above the river that offers a commanding view. William Gillette,

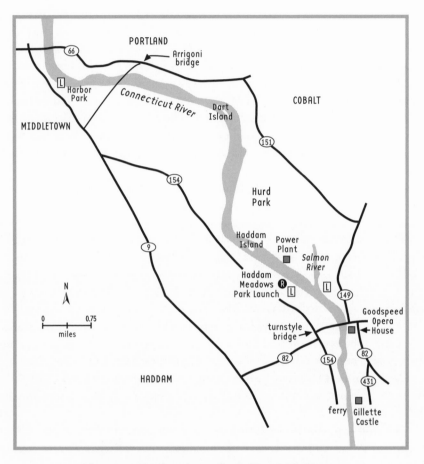

MIDDLETOWN, CONN., TO EAST HADDAM, CONN.

who in 1913 anchored his houseboat in the river and gazed up at the ridge, selected the site for the castle. He soon purchased the hill and designed his own twenty-four-room castle, complete with a secret room on the third floor with a window and fireplace for whenever he wished to be alone. Although the entire structure looks like a sand castle, the walls are a bit sturdier: four feet thick and made of locally harvested granite, shale, sandstone, and quartz. With walls like that you can't have flimsy doors, so Gillette designed massive gothic-looking wooden doors complete with interlocking mechanisms. (Inspiration for the castle came from the Normandy fortress of Robert LeDiable, father of William the Conqueror.) Construction of the castle cost Gillette a million dollars; being the actor who portrayed Sherlock Holmes more than 1,300 times, he had amassed a fortune and the castle was to be his retirement home. He also was smart enough to care what happened to his beloved castle after his death. His will states that his heirs must "see to it that the property does not fall into hands of some blithering saphead."

Gillette Castle is now owned by the state and part of Gillette Castle State Park. The castle is open to the public in the warm weather months and the surrounding forest trails are open year-round. Hiking trails follow an old miniature railroad bed constructed by Gillette. He called it the Seventh Sister Shortline, and he would treat his guests to a ride while he operated the throttle.

On a prior visit I stood on the castle's patio overlooking the river, hoping to see one of the bald eagles known to frequent the area. I began talking to a construction worker who was doing renovations to the castle when he said, "Did you see that?"

"See what?" I asked.

"A bald eagle just swooped over the patio, right behind your head."

I may have missed that eagle, but later that winter I saw more than a dozen on a boat cruise looking for bald eagles. The eagles congregate on the Connecticut River during the winter and the best way to see them is by boat. Fortunately, the Deep Water Navigation Company runs an excursion boat, the *Cross Rip*, on an eagle watch cruise every Saturday beginning in mid-January and continuing through mid-March. The three-hour cruise takes passengers on a circular route from Essex northward to East Haddam.

During my trip the ride upstream produced only a couple of eagle sightings at far distances, but on the downstream ride we saw eighteen birds, three of which were perched in trees next to the riverbank. The first close-up sighting occurred opposite the Goodspeed Opera House. It was an adult eagle with a distinctive white head and white tail separated by dark plumage. I clicked away with my camera as the bird took wing and glided over the river toward the hilltop ridge flanking the east bank. What a thrill! For years I've been trying to get pictures of bald eagles, and finally I had my first shot where a viewer could actually see the bird's magnificent features rather than a black speck in the sky. Best of all the eagle was framed by a crystal blue sky with no foliage from a tree to mar the shot.

Bald eagles winter on the Connecticut because much of the river remains ice free. These fierce-looking birds with hooked bills feed primarily on fish, but will also take waterfowl and small mammals with their strong talons. They are notorious thieves, often swooping down on other birds of prey and harassing them until they drop their catch, which the eagle promptly carries off. In the winter the bald eagle can also be seen scavenging on dead carcasses on the ice.

Although the eagle has made a dramatic comeback since the banning of the pesticide DDT, it still faces threats from human activities such as loss of habitat due to development, disturbance of nest sites, electrocution from power lines, and collision injuries. Eagles are easily upset by humans and tend to make their nests at secluded sites, such as the Quabbin Reservoir and the wilds of northern Maine and Canada.

The next eagle sighting occurred at Rich and Lord Islands. The eagles were circling above the islands, far up in the sky, and I elected to stay in

The Goodspeed Opera House, a six-story victorian building constructed just after the Civil War, graces the river with its beauty.

the cabin of the boat where a small heater took the bite out of the air. But at Seldon Island another mature bird was perched in a dead snag, and I scrambled up top, shivering in below-zero temperatures. Seldon Island, used by the eagles for night roosting, is one of the biggest islands on the Connecticut, approximately two-miles long and a half-mile wide. At one time Seldon island was a peninsula, but a storm lengthened a channel on its eastern side, called Seldon Creek; it's now possible to canoe down the creek and around the island. (Because bigger boats cannot navigate the narrow, shallow creek, local boaters tell me it has some fine largemouth bass fishing.)

As the *Cross Rip* cruised downriver, we occasionally came upon frozen sections where the boat plodded through mini icebergs, shattering small pieces of ice skimming over the larger flows. With a cup of hot cocoa in hand, I enjoyed watching the sailing shards of ice and the creaking sound they made. Countless coves looked inviting for springtime exploration, but one of the crew gave me the same advice as Al: only do my paddling on weekdays. "It gets a little squirrelly here on the weekends with all the motorboats," he explained. "That's why I love being on the water in the winter; you have the river all to yourself and the river is your focal point rather than worrying about boats."

I asked about the success rate of seeing eagles on the winter cruises and he said they have always had sightings. "On rare occasions we have even seen golden eagles and deer on Seldon Island." During my trip we saw red-tailed hawks, golden eye, mergansers, swans, and geese. One of the most memorable sights was a group of forty cormorants roosting in a tree hanging over the river.

I would have missed spotting the last eagle of the day without the help of the Audubon guide who narrated the trip. It was an immature eagle, without the white head, and its plain brown coloring blended in with the tree in which it was perched. Even though the bird was three feet tall, it was next to impossible to distinguish from the trees and branches. Being all one color the eagle seemed rather dull until it took to the air, soaring on a wingspan of six feet. No wonder the eagle was chosen as our national symbol over the objections of Benjamin Franklin—who preferred the wild turkey!

15

East Haddam, Connecticut, to the Sea

A week after my ride with Al, I decide to return and paddle the coves and inviting sections of the river. Below Gillette Castle is a launch site adjacent to the Chester-Hadlyme ferry, and I set out in my kayak for Seldon Island.

It's about a mile of paddling downriver to the island and along the way I pass Whalebone Creek, some nice sandy beaches, and a retaining wall along the riverbank. A new mansion overlooks the river with a large dock, complete with "Keep Out" sign; a simple "Private Property" posting would suffice rather than such a strong message of exclusion. I turn into the mouth of Seldon Creek, checking out an island campsite overlooking the creek. A family is enjoying a cookout by the campfire, looking like the picture-perfect outdoor scene—until the father picks up his cell phone.

The creek soon opens up into a large cove with several homes set back on the ridge. Egrets and a great blue heron stalk the shoreline, along with an angler, with whom I strike up a conversation. He tells me the creek usually has good bass fishing but today is slow. While we're talking I notice a nearby stump with shavings around it. Beaver. I had no idea beaver had made their way this far downriver.

The slow fishing later prompted me to call Bob Jacobs, Connecticut's Eastern District Supervisor of Fisheries, to learn more. "The striper fishing is really good," said Bob. "In May and June they are roaming in schools, although some will hold at structures such as rock piles where bait fish can be found. The bigger stripers are feeding on river herring, and live-lining herring is one of the more popular angling techniques."

I ask Bob about the Northern pike fishing, which I've heard is very good throughout the Haddam area. "Yes, it has improved," he says.

"It may be due in part to our rearing marsh at Haddam Meadow. In the late winter we introduce adult pike that are ready to spawn into the marsh. Once the young are born we begin to remove the adults—pike have no feelings for their family and are cannibalistic. Then we come back in June when the fingerlings are about four inches. We lower the water and trap them, releasing many into the Connecticut River. We have found that this technique decreases the mortality rate for the young. They grow very fast in the river, although they don't live as long as they might in other places. When they reach adulthood, the majority that are caught are in the five- to ten-pound range, with a few up to seventeen pounds." I ask him if the river shortened the pike's life span, and Bob explains that it is a fisheries phenomenon that the faster a fish grows the shorter its life. (I wonder if that applies to humans. I have seen a study saying that if you cut your calories significantly you live longer.)

❖ ❖ ❖

At the end of the cove I poke my kayak back into the creek, which is only about thirty feet wide, and pass through a junglelike tunnel of vines and trees. It's about a two-mile paddle down the creek, through low-lying marsh and woods, until I arrive at the southern end of Seldon Island and the river. For a few minutes I sit in the kayak wondering whether to take the creek back north or follow the river, making a complete loop. I hesitate to take the river because it is narrow, and even though it's a weekday, a fair amount of boaters are out. I finally elect to take my chances, but only because I'm in the kayak, which can handle the wakes better than a canoe and is twice as fast. The paddle north is a workout; not only are the waves rocking the kayak, but the wind is against me. It's a relief when I make it to the northern tip of the island and rest at a pine-shaded campsite called Hogback. This looks like the best campsite yet: fire pit, picnic tables, and a grassy slope leading to a granite ledge above the river. At night I'm sure it's nice and quiet, but right now the whine of personal watercraft roaring past ruins the mood. The riders do figure eights in the river and, even when they see me get back in the kayak and head their way, show no sign of slowing down. Finally, I holler out and ask them not to send wakes my way so I can paddle by.

Arriving at the ferry dock, I meet Charles Harlow, the ferryman, and decide to cross the river on the *Seldon II*. Charles invites me up to the wheelhouse where he's been piloting the boat for the past twenty-two years.

"We operate from April through November," Charles explains, "and with the price of gas going up, more and more locals are using the ferry rather than driving the extra miles up to the bridge at the Goodspeed Opera House. The ferry has been operating since 1768 and we get a fair amount of tourists who want to take the ride on the weekends. That's also when the river traffic is at its peak—just two weeks ago a girl dumped her jet ski right in front of the ferry and I had to stop the boat or we would have run her

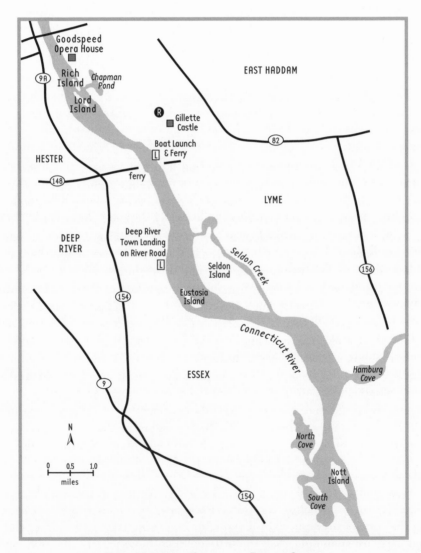

EAST HADDAM, CONN., TO ESSEX, CONN.

over. But weekday mornings, it's more relaxing. I see an occasional eagle and a couple times I've watched deer swim across the river."

I ask him about unusual passengers. "Oh," he chuckled, "that's easy. It had to be the guy from Yugoslavia. He had biked all the way here from Canada and was heading to New York to get passage on a ship to return to Europe. His only possession was a small backpack and a bike."

The ferry ride is a nice respite from the personal watercraft, a throwback to an unhurried way of life, and Charles seems as calm and unflappable as the river. When we reach Chester he wishes me well, and I drive south to Deep River Landing on the shore of the river opposite Seldon Island. A handsome gazebo rests on a point of land overlooking the Connecticut and the *Becky Thatcher* tour boat is moored nearby.

Deep River was once known for its ivory products such as combs, buttons, and finished keyboards. These goods were shipped out each night on the Hartford-to-New York steamboat, which made daily stops here for passenger service from 1845 until 1931. The ivory trade was so successful that elephant tusks shipped from Zanzibar arrived at Deep River Landing at a rate of 12,000 pounds per month. Shipbuilding was the other trade at Deep River, and sloops, schooners, and other vessels were manufactured here between 1793 and 1867. A sign at the landing says that a 400-ton brig launched in 1861 was named *Music* in honor of the piano keys made here.

I explore some of the back roads through the town, particularly Essex Street and River Road, which pass beautiful homes overlooking the river. At the center of Deep River people have gathered to listen to a band, and I notice the Riverwind Inn. I decide I'm too relaxed to break the spell by driving home to Massachusetts and check in at the Inn. Barbara Barlow, the owner, meets me at the door and gives me a quick tour. Every room is loaded with antiques, from clawfoot bathtubs to pine armoires and comb-painted chests. Four of the guest rooms have fireplaces and the eighteenth-century keeping room has a massive twelve-foot stone cooking fireplace. After a day on the river this is the perfect spot to rest.

❖ ❖ ❖

At dawn I decide to paddle the coves of Essex before the boaters awake. I think I have South, Middle, and North Coves all to myself, until I realize I've got company under the water. The surface ripples in various places as if sea serpents lurk below. My initial guess is striped bass or seals are causing the commotion, but when I cruise over to a big swirl, it becomes clear that carp are spawning. Not the little goldfish-bowl variety, the two- and three-footers roll on the surface like submarines breaking to the top.

One particularly big carp is so interested in the opposite sex, I'm able to paddle quietly next to it.

Next I observe a mute swan. These large white birds are exotics from Europe and I discover they will hold their ground. Without realizing I have encroached on their territory, the swan turns toward the kayak, hissing at me. Then I notice her chicks back at the edge of the marsh grass and I leave them in peace. Later I watch another mute swan take off, seeing how it uses its feet as if running while its wings flap furiously. It takes a long time for a bird that big to get airborne.

I paddle to the outlet of South Cove at Hayden Point, amazed at the power of the outgoing tide pulling my kayak into the river proper. A twenty-foot steel warning light sits on a rock base and on the top an osprey has made its nest. The bird must be used to kayakers and boaters because it barely even looks my way. While the outgoing tide carries massive volumes of water to the sea, the incoming tide brings salt water into the fresh water of the river and coves, making them brackish. The salt content is only about one-fifth of what it is at the mouth of the river, but it still limits the species of wetland plants to about thirty-five. Upriver, where the coves are entirely fresh water, live over 100 different varieties of plants.

Yachts of every imaginable size are moored in Essex. Bobbing along in my little kayak, I notice that for every boat owner lounging in a deck chair another is working hard painting, fueling, etc.

I wander over to a handsome white building that was a steamboat warehouse in the 1800s and now houses the Connecticut River Museum. Inside are exhibits chronicling the history of the river, including 12,000-year-old quartz projectile points, finely detailed ship models, and twentieth century paintings of life on the Connecticut. But the most fascinating exhibit is the *American Turtle*, a full-scale working model of the world's first submarine.

David Bushnell, who tested his submarine off Ayer's Point on the Connecticut River in the summer of 1775, built the original *Turtle*. Prior to the construction of the *Turtle*, Bushnell had developed and successfully exploded an underwater mine. To make the mine useful it needed a method of delivery, and Bushnell began construction of his submarine. Rather than the long, sleek submarines we know today, the *Turtle* was oval shaped and barely big enough to hold one person inside. The oak-beam casings resembled two joined turtle shells.

How could such a contraption sink a much larger ship? Step one was to maneuver the *Turtle* beneath an enemy craft. On the top of the *Turtle* was a sharp iron screw that was driven into the hostile ship's bottom and detached from the submarine. Then, explosives were attached and activated with a timer. When the *Turtle* neared the surface, fresh air was drawn into the craft via a tube with a floating ball near its inverted outlet that would ride up with any waves and seal the opening from the water. If the submarine needed to rise quickly, it could drop a 200-pound segment of its outer ballast. Manually operated propellers gave the submarine power and a rudder was used for steering. Navigation was possible through the phosphorescent tips of a compass and a depth gauge.

The Connecticut River Museum houses a full-scale working model of the world's first submarine.

During the Revolution there were high hopes for the *Turtle's* effectiveness against the British fleet, including an endorsement from Benjamin Franklin who had witnessed the *Turtle's* test runs on the Connecticut River. But the *Turtle* was ill-fated from the start. On its first mission in New York harbor, Ezra Bushnell, David's brother and the original operator, fell ill. A replacement hastily had to be summoned to guide the *Turtle* toward the intended target: Admiral Lord Howe's flagship, the *Eagle*. The new operator's lack of skill spelled failure as it did on two other attempts. (The real wonder is that the operator survived being submerged in the *Turtle*.) Eventually the *Turtle* itself was sunk when the ship transporting it was hit by enemy fire.

Bushnell was not finished, however, and he began developing drift mines made with a series of exposed wheels tipped with sharp iron points. These proved more successful than the *Turtle*. The enemy frigate, *Cerberus*, sailed by one such mine, which was spotted by the seamen on board. Curiosity proved to be their curse. The seamen began hauling up the mine, and when its wheel dragged against the ship's hull it set the charge in motion, blowing the ship to pieces.

During a raid on Norwalk, Bushnell was captured by the British, but was later traded for English prisoners and released. He then dropped out of sight, changed his name to Dr. Bush, and resurfaced in Georgia, beginning a new life as a physician.

❖ ❖ ❖

After walking through Essex, with its clapboard houses and eighteenth-century feel, I lunch at the Black Seal and then drive the last few miles to the mouth of the river in Old Lyme, on the opposite side of the river. One would think the entrance to a 410-mile-long river would be totally developed, but, because of the sandbar at the river's mouth, deep-draft ships are unable to navigate up the river. Consequently, there is no port city but rather a broad estuary left largely unspoiled by humans. In 1993, The Nature Conservancy designated the tidelands of the Connecticut River one of forty Last Great Places in the hemisphere, recognizing its pristine and complex ecological systems. The river's estuary was also named a Wetland of International Importance under the Ramsar Convention International Treaty—one of only fifteen such designations in the United States.

Perhaps the best places to experience this natural gem are at Griswold Point and Great Island. The mile-long sand spit known as Griswold Point is a great place to get acquainted with the tidelands on foot. The piping plover is on the list of state and federal threatened species and it lives and nests on sandy beaches such as Griswold Point. At low tide these small wading birds feed at the surf's edge. Piping plovers can be identified by a black stripe across their foreheads and a yellow beak with a black tip. Their nests are made in the sand of the beach and are easily disturbed.

Nesting areas of the beach are off-limits during the nesting season that runs May through June. (The lower Connecticut hosts several rare plants and animals, including forty-four species listed under the Connecticut Endangered Species Act.)

Launching from Smith's Neck Road in Old Lyme, you can see several osprey: their high pitched, piercing cry is unmistakable.

For my final paddle I choose the launch at Smith's Neck Road in Old Lyme, where Great Island protects backwater estuaries from the main stem of the river. Kayakers or canoeists at Smith's Neck can choose between a short one-and-a-half hour Southern Trail, or the longer three-hour Northern Trail. The Southern Trail leads to Griswold Point, while the Northern Trail winds through an inland waterway northward to Watch Rock, thought to be a Native American lookout point. Both trails pass by Great Island and through the sprawling marsh. There are many creeks and channels to explore. Snowy egrets and great blue herons are two of the larger birds that hunt here. Also seen are northern diamond-backed terrapins, a turtle found in brackish waters.

The area was extensively ditched during the 1930s in an effort to control mosquito populations, although some of the ditches date as far back as the Civil War. Early settlers made good use of the marsh, and harvested the salt hay. This hay was used for livestock bedding so better quality hay could be saved for feeding.

When I launch, only one other kayaker is enjoying the maze of passages through the tidelands. First I head north up the Back River,

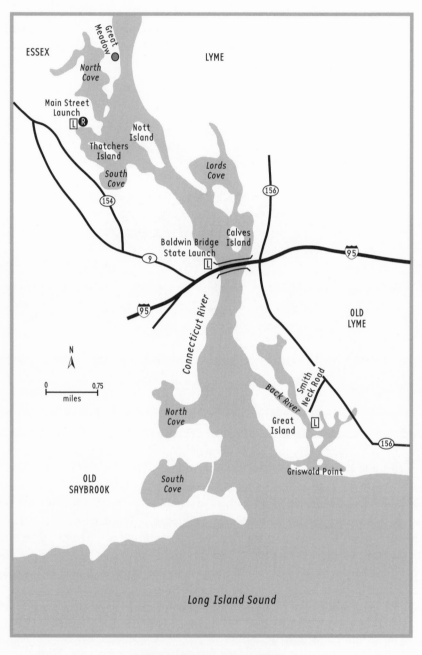

ESSEX, CONN., TO THE SEA

watching the osprey soar overhead. Several osprey poles have been erected and these fish hawks are often seen hunting along the marsh, bringing fish back to the nest. Their high-pitched, piercing cry is unmistakable: a kind of coastal call of the wild evoking the same awe as the loon's wail on inland lakes or the coyote's howl in the mountains.

The partial recovery of the osprey population is a direct result of the banning of the pesticide DDT in the 1970s. Prior to the chemical's discontinuance, DDT was used as a mosquito control in the salt marshes and was absorbed by microorganisms. Fish that fed upon the microorganisms ingested it, and the toxin worked its way up the food chain when the osprey preyed upon the fish. When the osprey laid their eggs, the effects of DDT thinned the shells resulting in low breeding success.

Other threats to the osprey include the loss of wetlands to development and the increase in raccoons, which raid osprey nests. Special poles and elevated platforms for nesting sites have helped in overcoming the problem of predators. Land protection efforts are helping protect the wetlands and maintain viable osprey habitats. Be careful not to disturb an osprey, especially one caring for eggs or chicks. The presence of people can cause the osprey to fly, leaving their nest unprotected to predators and other harm.

I planned to kayak a couple of miles up the estuary to Watch Rock, but every now and then the strong scent of the ocean comes to me on a breeze and it's simply too much of a lure to ignore. I turn back south and soon, at the pass between Great Island and Griswold Point, I feel the tug of the outgoing tide sweeping my kayak toward a line of small breakers at the river's mouth. Pulling up at the shore, I hop out and lie on the sand, listening to lapping waves, screaming gulls, and the distant horn of a passing ship. I can see two lighthouses directly across the river: Saybrook Lighthouse is the inner one and the Saybrook Jetty Lighthouse is the outer one. Unseen but somewhere beneath the sand and surf are the remains of a mysterious wooden ship, found in 1994 then subsequently covered by a coastal storm in 1996. So many layers of history began and ended here.

The end of the river seems as special and lonely as the source, and I think back on some of my favorite days exploring the river. I remember the hike with my brother Mark to Fourth Connecticut Lake, the giant bull moose, and my solo paddle through Colebrook where I took my first of many swims in the river. Then there was the trout Cogs and I cooked on the river in Guildhall, followed by the paddle through a pitch-black night trying to reach my car. Some of my most vivid memories are not of paddling but of camping, like the flood that swept through Orford, and a couple of solitary nights I spent in a farmer's field where I was allowed to pitch my tent after a day on the river. I remember the boater who tried to run me down by the Fort at Number Four, and the disappointment of seeing how crowded the river could be on weekends even in southern Vermont. This, of course, was followed by elation when paddling through the secluded shallows near Sunderland. I smile thinking of my son's face when he caught the big smallmouth in Hatfield, of our swinging from the riverside rope, and of our relaxing night at the Clark Tavern. Farther down in Northampton, I still can see Big Bill laughing in the pouring rain when I show him the dinosaur tracks. The early morning paddles through Springfield and Hartford come flooding back, where I felt like a thief paddling unseen through the sleeping cities. More recently there was the joy of being a passenger on Al's boat and the thrill of spotting the bald eagles on the winter trip. But mostly I'm thinking ahead, thinking of future trips on the Connecticut now that I understand the river a bit better than before.

The end of the river seems as special and lonely as the source.

Explorer's Notes

The following exploration suggestions include all the helpful tips and telephone numbers not found in the text. Launch sites generally are shown on the chapter maps, but directions to difficult-to-find launch sites (particularly in more populated towns downriver) are also outlined here. *Remember: everything is subject to change.*

Chapter 1

Sights to See

- The source: At the custom station on the U.S.–Canadian border, ask directions to the source of the Connecticut River (Fourth Connecticut Lake). The trail is steep in spots and takes about thirty-five minutes.

- Suggested moose watching: Along Route 3 at dawn and dusk between First Connecticut Lake and Second Connecticut Lake. Look for moose in the swampy areas.

- Magnetic Hill is located at the base of the first hill over the Canadian border on Route 3 (about one mile over the border).

- Suggested bird watching: Third Connecticut Lake on Route 3, Scott Bog (just southeast of Third Connecticut Lake), and East Inlet (drains into Second Connecticut Lake). Third Connecticut Lake has a sandy beach for swimming at its northern end, and nearby on the northwest shore you can step over the three-foot-wide Connecticut River where it flows into the lake. Scott Bog is a relatively shallow lake, about a mile long, and is quite secluded. East Inlet, a narrow pond, is a fascinating body of water to explore.

- Magalloway Tower: Look for a sign on Route 3 at a side road (east side) just north of First Connecticut Lake. Take this road (careful: it's rough in spots) and follow the signs about eight miles to a parking area. It's a forty-minute hike to the tower (3,360 feet in elevation). Great views.

- Old-growth forest: Although humans have not tampered with this section of forest, the spruce budworm infestation of 1974–1982 killed many of the trees. Still, it's nice to see a place that has been left untouched. The Nature Conservancy now owns it. Drive past the East Inlet Dam for 2.5 miles then take the left fork. Hike past the remains of an old bridge and what's left of the old-growth forest will be on your left.

- Covered bridge: Located near the confluence of Perry Stream and the Connecticut River.

Fishing

- Fishing license regulations: For residents of Vermont and New Hampshire, either states' fishing license is valid on the Connecticut River for its entire length. For out-of-staters, you need a New Hampshire license to fish anywhere on the river east of the Vermont low-water mark.

- Trout fishing access on foot: At the confluence of Perry Stream and the Connecticut River below First Connecticut Lake, the Connecticut River below Second Connecticut Lake, and the Connecticut River below Lake Francis. Several sections are fly-fishing only.

- Lake fishing: Trout fishing in Third, Second, and First Connecticut Lakes as well as Lake Francis. Landlocked-salmon fishing in Second and First Connecticut Lakes and Lake Francis.

Lodging and Camping in Pittsburg

- North Country Chamber of Commerce: 603-237-8939

- The Glen: 603-538-6500 (winter: 508-475-0559)

- Timberland Lodge and Cabins: 800-545-6613

- Ramblewood Ranch and Cabins: 603-538-6948

- Partridge Lodge: 603-538-6380

- Tall Timber Lodge: 800-83-LODGE, 800-835-6343 (in state: 603-538-6651)

- Lopstick Lodge and Cabins: 800-538-6659 (in state: 603-538-6659)

- Lake Francis State Park Campground: 603-538-6965

- Spruce Cone Cabins and Campground: 800-538-6361 (in state: 603-538-6361)

- Deer Mountain Campground: (formerly Moose Falls Campground) is state operated and located just north of Second Connecticut Lake, 603-271-3628.

CHAPTER 2

Sights to See

- Monadnock Mountain is reached on the Vermont side of the river, downstream from the Colebrook bridge and up a farm lane between two houses.

- Be sure to visit the Columbia covered bridge, a truly peaceful spot. Signs will direct you there from both the Vermont and New Hampshire sides of the river (see map in Chapter 2).

Fishing

- A catch and release trout fishing section begins 1,600 feet upstream from Bloomfield/North Stratford bridge and runs to a point 250 feet below the Lyman Dam. The dam is located about three miles above the North Stratford bridge.

- Although the river is "owned" by New Hampshire (via old laws) and New Hampshire regulations apply, fishing licenses for either Vermont or New Hampshire are acceptable.

Guide Services

- Lisa Wheeler Guide Service: 800-538-2448

- Osprey Fishing Charters: 603-922-3800

- Durcrets Sporting Goods, 140 Main Street, Colebrook, rents canoes and sells fishing licenses: 603-237-4900

Lodging and Camping:

• Colebrook Country Club Motel (Colebrook): 603-237-5566

• Monadnock Bed and Breakfast (Colebrook): 603-237-8216

• Guildhall Bed and Breakfast (Guildhall): 802-676-3720

• Maidstone Lake campsites: Maidstone State Park has campsites near the clean, cold waters of Maidstone Lake. Where the road forks a couple miles up Paul Stream from the Connecticut, veer away from the stream and head to Maidstone Lake.

CHAPTER 3

Guide Services

• Vermont Waterways Guided Canoe and Kayaking Trips: 800-492-8271

Boat Rentals

• Eastern Mountain Sports (canoe rentals in West Lebanon): 603-298-7716

• Ledyard Canoe Club (Dartmouth): 603-643-6709

Lodging and Camping

• Loch Lyme Lodge (Lyme): 800-423-2141

• A Century Past Bed and Breakfast (Newbury): 802-866-3358

• Breakfast on the Connecticut (Lyme): 603-353-4444

• Longmeadow Inn (East Ryegate): 800-394-2538

• Inn at Maplemont Farm (Barnet): 800-230-1617

• McIndoe Falls Inn (McIndoe): 800-782-9462

• Norwich Inn (Norwich): 802-649-1143

• Vaughan Meadow campsite (South Newbury): Located about one mile below the stone abutment of the former Bedell bridge. Look for the campsite on a wooded bank above a small curving beach. Operated by the Upper Valley Land Trust: 603-643-6626 or www.uvlt.org.

CHAPTER 4

Sights to See

• Wilder Dam Visitors Center: Take Route 5 in Wilder, Vermont, to Depot Street (on the right if you're heading north at the post office). Follow Depot Street to the first left on Norwich Street, then turn right onto Passumpsic Avenue. It is open from 10 A.M. to 6 P.M., Memorial Day through Columbus Day weekend.

Boat Rentals

• Fairlee Marine: 802-333-9745

Lodging and Camping

• Pastures Campground (Route 10 in Orford): 603-353-4579

• Silver Maple Lodge (Fairlee): 802-333-4326

• Chieftan Motor Inn (Hanover): 800-443-7024

• Bradford Motel (Bradford): 802-222-4467

• Alden Inn (Lyme): 800-794-2296

• Connecticut On The River Inn (Lyme): 603-353-4444

• Birch Meadow campsite: Located two miles below the arch bridge in Fairlee, Vermont. Look for the low, wooded point just above the marsh land at the outlet from Lake Morey. Operated by the Upper Valley Land Trust: 603-643-6626 or www.uvlt.org.

• Roaring Brook campsite: The campsite is on Palmer Farm in North Thetford, Vermont, and is located on the outside of a left river bend where Roaring Brook enters the Connecticut. Operated by the Upper Valley Land Trust: 603-643-6626 or www.uvlt.org

• Thetford campsite: Just past a stone bridge abutment near North Thetford, the river is bordered by a straight wooded section on the Vermont side. The campsite is located along this wooded stretch. Operated by the Upper Valley Land Trust: 603-643-6626 or www.uvlt.org.

CHAPTER 5

Sights to See

• American Precision Museum (South Main Street, Windsor, Vermont): 802-674-5781

• Saint-Gaudens National Historic Site (Cornish): 603-675-2175; open May through October.

• Sumner Falls: Access is via an unnamed dirt road in Hartland, Vermont, where Route 5 crosses beneath Interstate 91.

Boat Rentals

• North Star Canoe Rentals: 603-542-5802 (They will bring you to the launch site and you can canoe back to North Star Rentals.)

Guide Services

• John Marshal (fly fishing): 802-457-4021

• Marty Bannak (fly fishing): 802-295-7620

• David Deen (fly fishing): 802-869-3116

Lodging and Camping

• Chase House Bed and Breakfast (Cornish): 800-401-9455

• Radisson Hotel (Lebanon): 800-794-2296

• Wilgus State Park (camping along the Connecticut River in Weathersfield, Vermont): 802-886-2434 or 802-674-5422

• Burnap's Island campsite: Located three miles below the mouth of the Mascoma River and the interstate highway bridge at West Lebanon, and just above the mouth of the Ottauquechee River. Access is from the west side of the island off the main channel. Operated by the Upper Valley Land Trust: 603-643-6626 or www.uvlt.org.

• Burnham Meadow campsite: Located near Boston Brook, four miles below Sumner Falls and one mile below Hart Island. Just below the campsite, the river bends to the east and a railroad embankment follows the shore. Operated by the Upper Valley Land Trust: 603-643-6626 or www.uvlt.org.

Chapter 6

Sights to See

• Fort at Number Four (Charlestown, New Hampshire): 603-826-5700; open daily, Memorial Day weekend through late October, 10 A.M. to 4 P.M.

Lodging and Camping

• Maple Hedge Bed and Breakfast (Charlestown): 603-826-5237

• Horsefeathers Inn (Bellows Falls): 802-463-9776

• Baker Road Inn (Springfield): 802-886-2304

• Bull Run Bed and Breakfast (Springfield): 802-886-8470

Chapter 7

Sights to See

• Vernon Dam Fish Viewing Window: open 8 A.M. to 8 P.M. seasonally.

• Vermont Yankee Nuclear Power Plant: The power plant has an information center on Governor Hunt Road in Vernon, just outside the gates of the plant. It has exhibits, energy-related computer games, and visitors can generate their own electricity on a bicycle generator. Attached to the information center is the 200-year-old residence of Vermont's former lieutenant governor, Jonathan Hunt, which is open to the public. Tours of the atomic plant are available for people age eighteen and over by appointment; call 802-258-5796.

• Rudyard Kipling's Estate (Naulakha): 802-254-6868

Boat Rentals

• Vermont Canoe Touring Center (Brattleboro): 802-257-5008

Boat Launch

• One-fourth of a mile north of the bridge connecting Walpole to Westminster on the Walpole side, off Route 12. A dirt road leads to a car-top boat launch.

Lodging and Camping

- Monadnock, New Hampshire, Region Chamber of Commerce: 603-352-1303

- Brattleboro Chamber of Commerce: 802-254-4565

- Brattleboro North KOA: 802-562-5905

- Hidden Acres Camping (Brattleboro): 802-254-2098

- Fort Dummer State Park and Camping (Brattleboro): 802-254-2610

CHAPTER 8

Sights to See

- Northfield Mountain Recreation and Environment Center: 413-659-3714. Offers hiking and biking trails, tours of the power-generating operation, nature programs, and exhibits.

- Quinnetukut II Tour Boat: 413-659-3714 or 800-859-2960

- Turners Falls Fishway: Located on First Street just south of the Turners Falls bridge.

- Great Falls Discovery Center: An interpretive center focusing on the natural and cultural history of the Connecticut River. Also the headquarters for the Silvio O. Conte National Wildlife Refuge. Located in the center of Turners Falls across from the town hall; call 413-863-3221.

Boat Rentals

- Taylor Rental (Greenfield): 413-773-6843

- Barton Cover Camping and Canoe Rentals: 413-863-9300

Lodging and Camping

- About two dozen hotels, motels, bed and breakfasts, and camp-grounds are in Deerfield, Whately, Erving, and Greenfield: call the Franklin County Chamber of Commerce at 413-773-5463.

- Munns Ferry campsite is on a first-come, first-served basis with no fee. It has an Adirondack shelter, five tent sites, water, and pit toilets.

CHAPTER 9

Sights to See

• Mount Sugarloaf State Reservation has trails to the summit and an access road that is open seasonally; call 413-545-5993. The access road can be reached from Route 5 in South Deerfield.

• Mohawk Trail State Forest (6,457 acres) is a thirty- to forty-minute drive west of Greenfield on Route 2; call 413-339-5504. Besides the steep trails up Todd Mountain and Clark Mountain, an old woods road runs along the Deerfield River, which is relatively flat.

Lodging and Camping

• White Birch Campground (Whately): 413-665-4941

• For a complete list of accommodations and campsites, call the Franklin County Chamber of Commerce at 413-773-5463.

CHAPTER 10

Boat Rentals

• Sportsman's Marina rents canoes, fishing boats with outboards, and pontoon boats: 413-586-2426

• Wildwater Outfitters (Route 9 in Hadley) rents canoes and kayaks: 413-586-2323

• Eastern Mountain Sports (Hadley) rents one canoe and one kayak: 413-584-3554

Lodging and Camping

• Clark Tavern: 413-586-1900

• Franklin County Chamber of Commerce: 413-773-5463

CHAPTER 11

Sights to See

• Porter-Phelps-Huntington Historic House Museum: Route 47 in Hadley, 413-584-4699

• Norwottuck Rail Trail: An 8.5-mile paved pathway that runs from Northampton to Amherst. Access is available at Elwell Recreation

Area (just off Interstate 91 at Exit 18 on Damon Road in Northampton), Station Road in Amherst, or at the Mountain Farms Mall in Hadley—3.7 miles east of the Connecticut River bridge on Route 9.

• Elwell Recreation Area: Offers a rowing program for people with disabilities. For more information, call the Connecticut River Greenway State Park at 413-586-8706.

• Floodplain Forest Reserve: A large protected floodplain with silver maple and cottonwood, some in excess of three feet in diameter. A blue-blazed trail leads through the woods. It can be reached from Route 47 at Mitch's Marina in Hadley by turning onto Hockanum Road, where a gate at an unpaved road leads to the hiking trail.

• The Dinosaur footprints: Can be reached by following Route 5 along the river north of Holyoke to a small parking pullout on the easterly side of the road. Follow the signed trail to the footprints and to the Connecticut River below. (The turnoff on Route 5 at the parking area is about five miles south of Exit 18 off Interstate 91.)

• Mount Holyoke: Part of Skinner State Park located along Route 47 in Hadley. The road leading to the summit is open from April through November, while hiking trails can be used year-round. The Summit House (also known as the Prospect House) is open on weekends from May to October. For park information, call 413-586-0350.

• Arcadia Wildlife Sanctuary: On Combs Road in Easthampton. This Audubon property covers 550 acres and includes frontage along the Connecticut River Oxbow. For information, call 413-584-3009.

Boat Rentals

• Sportsman's Marina rents canoes, fishing boats with outboards, and pontoon boats: 413-586-2426

• Wildwater Outfitters (Route 9 in Hadley) rents canoes and kayaks: 413-586-2323

• Eastern Mountain Sports (Hadley) rents one canoe and one kayak: 413-584-3554

Lodging and Camping

• Autumn Inn (Northampton): 413-584-7660

• The Inn at Northampton (Northampton): 800-582-2929

• The Knoll (Northampton): 413-584-8164

• Hotel Northampton (Northampton): 800-547-3529

• Grandmary's Bed and Breakfast (South Hadley): 413-533-7381

• For lodging and camping in Greater Springfield and Holyoke call
  the Greater Springfield Visitors Bureau at 800-723-1548.

Chapter 12

Sights to See

• Springfield's Connecticut River Cruise (Peter Pan River Bus):
  413-781-3320 or 800-343-9999

• Fanny Stebbins Wildlife Sanctuary/"The Meadows": From
  Interstate 91, take Exit 1 (Longmeadow) and follow Route 5
  south through town. Look for Bark Haul Road on the right at
  about the three-mile mark. Follow Bark Haul Road to where it
  ends at Pondside Road and park by the welcome sign.

• Hadley Falls Fishway: Traveling south on Interstate 91, take
  Exit 17 and make a left turn off of the exit ramp. Follow Dwight
  Street through downtown and over two canals, all the way to Race
  Street (about two miles), and turn left onto Race Street. Follow to
  the entrance of Hadley Falls Power Station on the left, just before
  the South Hadley Falls bridge. Traveling north of Interstate 91,
  take the Route 391 exit. Follow 391 until the Holyoke Main Street
  exit. Go right off the exit ramp onto Main Street (Route 116).
  Follow until the South Hadley bridge. Entrance to the fishway
  is on the left just before the bridge. The fishway opens in early
  May and visiting hours run Wednesday through Sunday. Peak
  viewing of shad is usually the end of May and the first week of
  June. Call 413-659-3714.

• Springfield Armory Museum: 413-734-6477, 1 Armory Square,
  Springfield: open Tuesday through Sunday, 10 A.M. to 4:30 P.M.

Lodging and Camping

- For lodging and camping in Greater Springfield and Holyoke, call the Greater Springfield Visitors Bureau at 800-723-1548.

CHAPTER 13

Sights to See

- Enfield Dam: Best viewed from a platform adjacent the parking area on Canal Street, located just south of Franklin Street.

- Luddy/Taylor Connecticut Valley Tobacco Museum: Northwest Park, 860-285-1888.

- Windsor Historical Society: Exhibits at one of the oldest frame houses in Connecticut; call 860-688-3813.

- Connecticut Audubon Center at Glastonbury: Includes exhibits on the Connecticut River ecosystem and trail system. Located at 1361 Main Street (Route 2, Exit 7); call 860-633-8402.

- The Mark Twain House: An elaborate mansion at 351 Farmington Avenue, 860-493-6411.

- Harriet Beecher Stowe House: A Victorian cottage with memorabilia, Farmington Avenue at Forest Street, 860-525-9317.

- Wethersfield Historical Society: A wide variety of exhibits, 150 Main Street, 860-529-7656.

- Wethersfield Nature Center: A 120-acre park with mammals, reptiles, and birds, 30 Greenfield Street, 860-721-2953.

- Museum of Connecticut History: Located in Hartford, the museum has changing exhibits along with permanent exhibits of Connecticut collections. Call 860-566-3056.

- Riverboat rides aboard the *Mark Twain*: Leave from the Charter Oak Landing, and are run by Deep River Navigation Company, 860-526-4954.

Boat Launches

- A launch is above the Enfield Rapids in Enfield. It is located on Asnuntuck Street off Pearl Street (near Main Street), about a half-mile up from the Suffield-Enfield Bridge. Lots of weekend traffic.

- Parson Road Boat Launch in Enfield is located one mile north of the junction of U.S. 5 and Interstate 91. Go west on Bridge Lane to Parson Road. Lots of weekend traffic.

- The Windsor launch is just south of the Windsor-South Windsor (Bissell) bridge. Turn east off Route 159 onto East Barber Street.

- Riverside Boat Launch in Hartford: From Interstate 91 take Exit 33 east on Jennings Road. Take the first right then the next left to Riverside Park. Crowded on weekends.

- Charter Oak Launch in Hartford: From Interstate 91 take Exit 27 and go east. Take the first left on Brainard Road, and then a left onto Reserve Road to the launch. Crowded on weekends.

Lodging and Camping

- Best Western Colonial Inn (East Windsor): 860-623-9411

- Classic Motel (East Windsor): 860-623-9411

- Charles Hart House Bed and Breakfast (Windsor): 860-688-5555

- Hosteling International-Windsor (Windsor): 860-683-4155

- Dozens of bed and breakfasts, hotels, motels, and campsites are available in Hartford, Glastonbury, Wethersfield, and East Hartford; call the Greater Hartford Tourism District at 800-793-4480.

Chapter 14

Sights to See

- Glastonbury-Rocky Hill Ferry: From Rocky Hill take Route 160 to Ferry Lane, and from Glastonbury take Main Street to Tyron Street.

- Dinosaur State Park: Exit 23 off Interstate 91 on West Street at Rocky Hill. Call 203-529-8423. Park is open daily from 9 A.M. to 4:30 P.M.

- Fall Foliage Riverboat Rides: Run by Deep River Navigation Company from the Harborpark Landing, 860-526-4954.

- Goodspeed Opera House: Offers musicals and tours, East Haddam, 860-873-8668.

- Gillette Castle: Open Memorial Day through Columbus Day, 10 A.M. to 5 P.M., 860-526-2336.

- Camelot Cruises: Offered from Marine Park (opposite Goodspeed Opera House) in Haddam. Cruises include a Murder Mystery Dinner Cruise, a New Orleans Dinner Cruise, Lunch and Dinner Cruises, an All Day Cruise, and a Foliage Cruise. Call 860-345-8591 for information.

Boat Launches

- Rocky Hill Ferry Launch Site: A day permit can be purchased when the attendant is on duty Saturday and Sunday between 8 A.M. and 7 P.M., or at the Rocky Hills Parks and Recreation Department.

- A boat launch is at the mouth of the Salmon River in East Haddam off Route 149, 1.5 miles north of the junction with Route 82.

- A boat launch is at East Haddam in Haddam Meadows State Park, east off Route 154.

Lodging and Camping

- For canoe camping in Connecticut, write the Department of Environmental Protection, Office of Parks and Recreation, Hartford, CT 06115, or call 860-424-3200 or 877-668-CAMP.

- Canoe Camping is allowed along the Connecticut River at Hurd State Park in East Haddam.

- Dozens of bed and breakfasts, hotels, and motels are available in Rocky Hill and Wethersfield; call the Greater Hartford Tourism District at 800-793-4480.

- Comfort Inn (Cromwell): 800-4-CHOICE

- Holiday Inn (Cromwell): 800-HOLIDAY

- Radisson Hotel (Cromwell): 800-333-3333

- Super 8 (Cromwell): 800-800-8000

- Bishopsgate Inn (East Haddam): 860-873-1677

- The Gelston House (East Haddam): 860-873-1411

- Klar Crest Resort (East Haddam): 860-873-8649

- Shanaghan's (East Haddam): 860-873-8283

CHAPTER 15

Sights to See

- Eagle Watch: For more information or to reserve a seat on the Cross Rip, call Deep River Navigation Company at 860-526-4954 or the Connecticut Audubon Society at 860-767-0660. The cruise departs from the town of Essex at the dock by the Connecticut River Museum.

- Deep River Navigation Company: Runs the Becky Thatcher Riverboat Ride and other riverboat cruises along the Saybrook waterfront. Or ride upriver from Saybrook to Essex aboard the Aunt Polly. Call Deep River Navigation Company at 860-526-4954.

- Deep River Landing: A gazebo and an observation deck overlooking the river—a great spot for a picnic.

- Connecticut River Museum: An historic dockhouse, exhibits, and replicas of the first submarine, 67 Main Street, Essex, 860-767-8296.

- Essex Steam Train and Riverboat Ride: Dine in an old-time dinner train with a 1920 steam engine. At Deep River Landing the train meets the boat for a one-hour cruise. Call 860-767-0103.

- The Stone House: In Deep River, this historic house has items relating to Connecticut River history. It is located on South Main Street.

- Connecticut River Valley and Shoreline Visitors Center: Call 800-486-3346.

Boat Launches

- In Hadlyme near the border of East Haddam and Lyme, just off Route 148 at the Chester-Hadlyme Ferry Crossing.

- Baldwin Bridge in Old Saybrook launch site: Take either Exit 1 or 2 off Route 9, and at the end of the exit go to Ferry Road beneath the Interstate 95 Bridge. Crowded on weekends.

- Town Park Boat Launch in Essex is for canoes and kayaks with access into the Essex Coves. Access is off Main Street in the municipal parking area behind the post office. It is a nice park with picnic benches.

- Lord Cove in Lyme has a launch site, but you must park your car a half-mile away in the park-and-ride lot just north of Interstate 95. To reach the launch site, take Exit 70 off Interstate 95 and drive north on Route 156 for about a half-mile to the town landing.

- Smith's Neck Launch and Griswold Point: Griswold Point can be reached by boat between Labor Day and Memorial Day. Paddling around Great Island is allowed anytime. To get to the Smith's Neck Boat Launch and onward to Griswold Point follow these directions: Take Interstate 95 to Exit 70. If northbound, turn right on Route 156 and go south for two miles. If southbound, turn left on Lyme Street and go 1.5 miles through Old Lyme, then turn left on Route 156 and continue for 0.3 mile. Turn right on Smith's Neck Road and follow it to the state boat launch at the end of the road. To continue on to Griswold Point, go past Smith's Neck Road to Old Shore Road, 1.5 miles on your right immediately after you cross the bridge over the Black Hall River. Follow Old Shore Road 0.4 mile to an unmarked road on the right with two stone pillars and a small sign for White Sands Beach. Take this right and follow the road to the end to a parking lot by the beach and park.

Lodging and Camping

- Call the Connecticut River Valley and Shoreline Visitors Council at 800-486-3346.

- Seldon Island Camping: Allow at least three weeks in advance for weekend reservations. Four primitive campsites are on the island, which are available by mail-in reservation only. Write to: River Camping, Gillette Castle State Park, 67 River Road, East Haddam, CT 06432, or call Gillette Castle at 860-526-2336. A few campsites are also by the water near the boat launch at Gillette Castle.

- Rocky Neck State Park in East Lyme: A number of campsites near the ocean. This is a beautiful state park with a beach on the Atlantic Shore; call 877-668-CAMP or 860-424-3200.

- Riverwind (Deep River): 860-526-2014

- Griswold Inn (Essex): 860-767-1776

- Hidden Meadow (Lyme): 860-434-8360

- Indian Ledge Bed and Breakfast (Lyme): 860-434-9566

- Bayberry Motor Inn (Old Lyme): 860-434-3024

- Bee & Thistle Inn (Old Lyme): 800-622-4946
- Old Lyme Inn (Old Lyme): 800-434-5352
- Saybrook Point Inn and Spa (Saybrook): 800-243-1212

KEEPING THE CONNECTICUT RIVER CLEAN AND SAFE

To prevent erosion and ensure safety, boats must not exceed headway speed (no wake, or six MPH) within 150 feet from shore, islands, bridges, other boats, swimmers, or floats.

Help prevent bank erosion by following speed rules, steering clear of exposed banks, leaving vegetation untouched, and not climbing steep banks. Respect the rights of riverfront landowners by carrying out all trash, asking permission before you cross private land, and parking your vehicle where it will not obstruct landowner access. Keep non-native species out of the river by not using bait, and wash your boat off or allow it to dry before launching in the river if you have used it in other bodies of water.

The Connecticut River's width and depth varies widely, and its flow can vary seasonally, daily, and even hourly. Currents can change dramatically with a rainstorm upstream or with the opening of gates at a dam. Use common sense. Boaters should check tides and weather forecasts before setting out.

❖   ❖   ❖

The headwaters of the Connecticut River originate in the 26-million-acre Northern Forest. The Northern Forest is the largest remaining wild forest in the East and supports a way of life cherished by generations of northern New England and New York residents. With the exception of

Lake Umbagog, the Upper Connecticut Lakes are the last large wild lakes in the Northern Forest region of New Hampshire. The area includes Second, Third, and Fourth Connecticut Lakes, and parts of Lake Francis and First Connecticut Lake. The New Hampshire Rivers Protection Project gave the Connecticut River's headwaters the highest possible score for critical ecological significance, inland fisheries, and scenic value, and both Indian and Perry Streams the highest score for undeveloped character. Unfortunately, continuous pressure to develop forest roads and available shorelines will take its toll on public access, water quality, and fisheries.

To find out more about what you can do to help protect the Connecticut River headwaters along with the rest of the Northern Forest, please contact:

Appalachian Mountain Club
Conservation Department
5 Joy Street
Boston, MA
(617) 523-0655
www.outdoors.org

Northern Forest Alliance
43 State Street
Montpelier, VT 05602
(802) 223-5265
www.thenorthernforest.org

Environmental Organizations

Connecticut River Joint Commissions (CRJC)
The states of Vermont and New Hampshire created the CRJC to preserve and protect the resources of the Connecticut River valley, and to guide its growth and development. The CRJC is active in many areas of valley life, including agriculture, heritage tourism, water quality, and recreation, and provides grants for local projects. CRJC can be reached at: P.O. Box 1182, Charlestown, NH 03603, 603-826-4800, or www.crjc.org.

Connecticut River Watershed Council (CRWC)
The Connecticut River Watershed Council was established in 1952 and is the only citizen group dedicated to the restoration and protection of the entire Connecticut River. Its two river stewards work at the community level to challenge inappropriate development and encourage river conservation. CRWC can be reached at 15 Bank Row, Greenfield, MA 01301, or at www.ctriver.org.

Upper Valley Land Trust (UVLT)
The Upper Valley Land Trust works to provide permanent protection of land and its resources, offering stewardship, education, and advice for the conservation and enhancement of agricultural, forested, recreational, and scenic lands. UVLT also has a guide to all primitive campsites along the river. For more information, contact UVLT at 19 Buck Road, Hanover, NH 03755, 603-643-6626, or www.uvlt.org.

Recommended Reading

Ambrose, Stephen E. *Undaunted Courage: Meriwether Lewis, Thomas Jefferson, and the Opening of the American West.* Simon & Schuster, 1996.

Bachman, Ben. *Upstream: A Voyage on the Connecticut River.* Boston, Mass.: Houghton Mifflin Company, 1985.

Borton, Mark, ed. *The Complete Boating Guide to the Connecticut River.* Easthampton, Mass.: The Connecticut River Watershed Council, 1986.

Cuneo, John. *Robert Rogers of the Rangers.* Ticonderoga, N.Y.: Fort Ticonderoga Museum, 1988.

Delaney, Edmund. *The Connecticut River.* Essex, Conn.: The Connecticut River Foundation, 1996.

Drake, Samuel. *The Old Indian Chronicle.* Boston, Mass.: Samuel Drake, Washington Street, 1867.

Dwelley, Marilyn. *Trees and Shrubs of New England.* Camden, Maine: Downeast Books, 1980.

Hard, Walter. *The Connecticut.* Lincoln, Mass.: Massachusetts Audubon, 1998.

Hill, Ralph. *Lake Champlain.* Woodstock, Vt.: Countryman Press, 1976.

Jas, Victoria, ed. *Appalachian Mountain Club River Guide: New Hampshire/ Vermont.* Boston, Mass.: Appalachian Mountain Club, 1983.

Johnson, Susanna. *A Narrative of the Captivity of Mrs. Johnson.* Springfield, Mass.: H.R. Hunting Company, 1814.

Jorgensen, Neil. *A Guide to New England's Landscape*. Chester, Conn.: The Pequot Press, 1977.

Rezendes, Paul. *Tracking and the Art of Seeing*. Charlotte, Vt.: Camden House Publishers, 1992.

Robinson, William F. *Abandoned New England*. Boston, Mass: New York Graphic Society, 1976.

Schultz, Eric, and Tougias, Michael. *King Philip's War*. Woodstock, Vt.: Countryman Press, 1999.

Stark, Caleb. *General John Stark and Biography of Captain Phineas Stevens*. Concord, N.H.: Edson Eastman, 1877.

Staubach, Suzanne. *Connecticut: Driving Through History*. North Attleborough, Mass.: Covered Bridge Press, 1998.

Thoreau, Henry David. *Journal*. New York, N.Y.: Bramhall House, 1852.

Verrill, Hyatt. *The Heart of Old New England*. New York, N.Y.: Dodd, Mead and Company, 1936.

Zirblis, Ray. "Was Samuel Morey Robbed?" *Vermont Life*, Autumn 1994.

ABOUT THE AUTHOR

Michael Tougias is the author of several books about New England including:

- ❖ *New England Wild Places* (Covered Bridge Press)
- ❖ *Autumn Rambles of New England* (Hunter Publishing)
- ❖ *Quiet Places of Massachusetts* (Hunter Publishing)
- ❖ *More Nature Walks in Eastern Massachusetts* (AMC Books)
- ❖ *Nature Walks in Central and Western Massachusetts* (co-authored with René Laubach, AMC Books)
- ❖ *Country Roads of Massachusetts* (Country Roads Press–NTC/Contemporary)
- ❖ *Exploring the Hidden Charles* (AMC Books)
- ❖ *A Taunton River Journey* (Taunton River Watershed Alliance)
- ❖ *King Philip's War: The History and Legacy of America's Forgotten Conflict* (co-authored with Eric Schultz, Countryman Press)
- ❖ *Until I Have No Country* (A novel of King Philip's Indian War, Covered Bridge Press)

Tougias gives narrated slide presentations for each of his books, including *River Days: Exploring the Connecticut River from Source to Sea*. If you are interested in his slide presentations or would like a brochure of all his books, please write to him at P.O. Box 72, Norfolk, MA 02056.

In his free time he leads visually impaired people on nature walks and is involved in protecting the open space in Massachusetts.

About the Appalachian Mountain Club

Since 1876, the Appalachian Mountain Club has helped people experience the majesty and solitude of the Northeast outdoors. We offer outdoor skills workshops, guided trips, and lodging options for all levels of outdoor adventuring. Our conservation programs include trail maintenance, air and water quality research, and conservation advocacy work to preserve the special outdoor places we love and enjoy for future generations.

Join the Adventure!

Take a hike, ride a bike, paddle a canoe. We believe that people who enjoy breathing fresh air, climbing mountains, splashing in streams, and walking on trails have more fun and take better care of the outdoors. Join the fun today. Call 617-523-0636 for membership information.

Outdoor Adventures

From beginner backpacking to advanced backcountry skiing, we teach outdoor skills workshops to suit your interest and experience. If you prefer the company of others and skilled leaders, we also offer guided hiking and paddling trips. Our four outdoor education centers guarantee year-round adventures.

Huts, Lodges, and Visitor Centers

With accommodations throughout the Northeast, you don't have to travel to the ends of the earth to see nature's beauty and experience unique wilderness lodging. Accessible by car or on foot, our lodges and huts are perfect for families, couples, groups, and individuals.

Books and Maps

We can lead you to the best hiking, biking, skiing, and paddling destinations from Maine to North Carolina. With more than 50 books and maps published, we're your definitive resource for discovering wonderful outdoor places. For ordering information call 800-262-4455.

Check us out online at **www.outdoors.org** for lots of great information.

Appalachian Mountain Club, 5 Joy Street,Boston, MA 02108-1490
617-523-0636

LEAVE NO TRACE

The Appalachian Mountain Club is a national educational partner of Leave No Trace, a nonprofit organization dedicated to promoting and inspiring responsible outdoor recreation through education, research, and partnerships. The Leave No Trace Program seeks to develop wildland ethics—ways in which people think and act in the outdoors to minimize their impacts on the areas they visit and to protect our natural resources for future enjoyment. Leave No Trace unites four federal land management agencies—the U.S. Forest Service, National Park Service, Bureau of Land Management, and U.S. Fish and Wildlife Service—with manufacturers, outdoor retailers, user groups, educators, organizations like the AMC and the National Outdoor Leadership School (NOLS), and individuals.

The Leave No Trace ethic is guided by these seven principles:

❖ Plan ahead and prepare.
❖ Travel and camp on durable surfaces.
❖ Dispose of waste properly.
❖ Leave what you find.
❖ Minimize campfire impacts.
❖ Respect wildlife.
❖ Be considerate of other visitors.

The AMC has joined NOLS—a recognized leader in wilderness education and a founding partner of Leave No Trace—as the sole national providers of the Leave No Trace Master Educator course through 2004. The AMC offers this five-day course, designed especially for outdoor professionals and land managers, as well as the shorter two-day Leave No Trace Trainer course at locations throughout the Northeast.

For Leave No Trace information and materials contact:

Leave No Trace
P.O. Box 997
Boulder, CO 80306
800-332-4100
www.LNT.org

SUPER SONS

what happened in book 2?

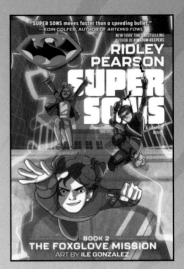

In *Super Sons: The Foxglove Mission* (Book 2), Jon Kent and Damian "Ian" Wayne (a.k.a. Superboy and Batkid) have teamed up to find out who poisoned Lois Lane and why. With the help of their friend Tilly, their investigation leads them to a group of women from Landis who call themselves "the Four Fingers"—they're determined to find Candace, another friend of Jon, Ian, and Tilly's.

Unfortunately for the Four Fingers, Candace—heir to the throne of Landis—has fled Wyndemere in search of her legacy. As she travels across the wildlands of a flooded Coleumbria, she learns more about who she is and the full extent of her powers.

But as she finally learns her truth, the Four Fingers catch up to her at the Coleumbrian Quarter, hoping she'll join their mission to poison the land with the same deadly virus infecting Lois.

Jon, Ian, and Tilly follow the Four Fingers to Candace, and they are able to locate where the virus is being mass-produced but can't destroy it.

Back in Wyndemere, infamous gang leader Avryc has escaped and is back to re-forming her relationship with the corrupt Coleumbrian politicians, Cray Ving, Sir Real, and G. Reed.

When the Super Sons team finally reaches Candace in battle with the Four Fingers, they help her fend off the villains, but not before the Four Fingers escape with a final sample of the virus. Now the Super Sons team must track the virus to Candace's homeland, Landis, where she can reclaim her throne and destroy the virus once and for all.

On to *Escape to Landis*...

DAMIAN "IAN" WAYNE

Ian doesn't know his mother. He wants to fight by the side of his father, Batman. He has no powers, but lots of gadgets. He is a bit conceited and critical of others. At thirteen years old he is quite independent, and seems older.

BRUCE WAYNE/BATMAN

Billionaire head of Wayne Enterprises (W.E.). His company builds the walls holding back the flood waters. As Batman, he secretly knows Superman. He is worried about the spreading illness and wants to find a cure.

PATIENCE

Bruce Wayne's assistant. She also looks after Ian Wayne when Bruce travels.

THE FOUR FINGERS

Four young women representing various districts in Landis. Their mission is to either stop Candace from being crowned empress, or to convince her to be different. Candace treats others as friends. The Four Fingers do not.

TACO

Ian Wayne's small but lovable dog. Ian considers Taco his best friend.

CANDACE

Candace was born in Landis, a continent far from the nation of Coleumbria. Her mother was an empress before she died. Now in possession of the special anointing oil, she is returning to Landis to be named empress and reclaim her land.

LOIS LANE
Mother of Jon Kent. Wife of Clark Kent. An important reporter for the *Daily Planet*. She was working on a big story about a spreading illness before becoming very ill. She knows Bruce Wayne.

CLARK KENT/SUPERMAN
Father of Jon Kent. Husband of Lois Lane. As Superman he is escorting a space expedition to Mars to help the PolarShield Project and save the planet.

JON KENT
Twelve-year-old Jon is the son of Clark Kent (Superman) and Lois Lane (reporter for the *Daily Planet* newspaper). While he can't fly, he can jump high and run fast, and his skin is pretty tough. He's optimistic, full of energy, and a team player.

PERRY WHITE
Lois and Clark's boss and the publisher of the *Daily Planet*.

JILL OLSEN
Lois Lane's assistant at the *Daily Planet*.

TILLY
Met Jon and Ian in school. Tilly is good with computers and all things mechanical. She's a crucial part of the Super Sons team.

A Guide to the
Characters and World of

SUPER
SONS

MRS. KIACK
Neighbor of the Kent family. She sometimes looks after Jon Kent when his parents are too busy, or are away on business.

SIR REALE

A politician and business-man who works for G. Reed. When something illegal needs to be done, he makes it happen so that it appears G. Reed isn't involved.

AVRYC

A powerful woman who controls gang members in Coleumbria. Bad people pay her and her gangs to do criminal things.

PARA SOL

Para Sol is a good person who runs the government's PolarShield Project. She works closely with Dr. Cray Ving (who's not so good!).

COLEUMBRIA

The world's most free democracy. A country with cities like Metropolis and Gotham and Wyndemere, as well as the capital city, the Coleumbrian Quarter. Climate disruption is flooding the country. Its citizens are moving inland to higher ground.

DR. CRAY VING

A scientist working for G. Reed. He is involved with the government's PolarShield Project to stop global warming.

WYNDEMERE

A large city in the north of Coleumbria on the shores of an enormous inland lake. Many residents of coastal cities are moving to Wyndemere.

LANDIS

A vast continent across the ocean that's controlled by an evil general.

Coleumbria General Hospital.

My mom's going to get better.

Of course she will.

Glad we were able to move her to the capital's hospital.

Mr. Wayne will find a cure to the virus.

And if he doesn't?

I can't just sit around and wait!

You must be careful, Jon. Lois was onto something big. Probably best not to get wrapped up in it.

15

19

21

27

33

34

35

36

42

44

45

47

49

51

53

Space and Flight Museum.

There's no time to stow away on a solar ship. And believe me, you'll never be allowed on a government solar plane.

That's why we asked for your help, Mr. Mylark.

Is there *any* way for us to get to Landis?

It's life and death.

My company supplies rations to our military around the world. Jon, you and Ian could hide inside a crate.

What about me?

Two will be tight. Three is impossible. I'm sorry, Tilly.

I understand. I can keep an eye on Mrs. Kent.

We're going to miss you, Til. We could really use the help.

62

63

67

We've been sitting in the same spot for three hours!

The Council instructed me to listen to the river.

A river brings life when it waters our fields, death when it floods our villages.

Hang on...I hear a whole bunch of fish swimming upstream toward us.

You can hear that? Amazing.

You've been out in the sun too long.

Ssh!

A thousand or more, forming... a line?

Tell me I'm seeing things!

Describe the image, please.

They look like a saw blade. Like the back of a dinosaur.

No...that looks like the Zeetqeest mountain range!

The fish didn't just happen to form a mountain range. So, what was that?

It also happened to me in Coleumbria. It carries two meanings for us.

First, our enemies, the Four Fingers, know we are here in Landis. Secondly, one of the four—whoever controls water animals—is secretly helping us.

We have a spy on our side!

Exactly!

Two days later...

The girl you described to me. She and two others left for the Zeetqeest Mountains two days ago. Across the desert this way.

Thank you so much!

Be careful, a dangerous group of warriors dwells in the desert. They are led by a fearsome woman, Talia al Ghul.

Talia? That name sounds familiar...

80

81

The Bat-Craft range is nine hundred miles. You will need to reach both Wayne Enterprises boats to recharge the Bat-Craft.
Some clothes and food and I'll be fine.
I'll find the boys, Patience. I'll warn them. And I'll get them home!

101

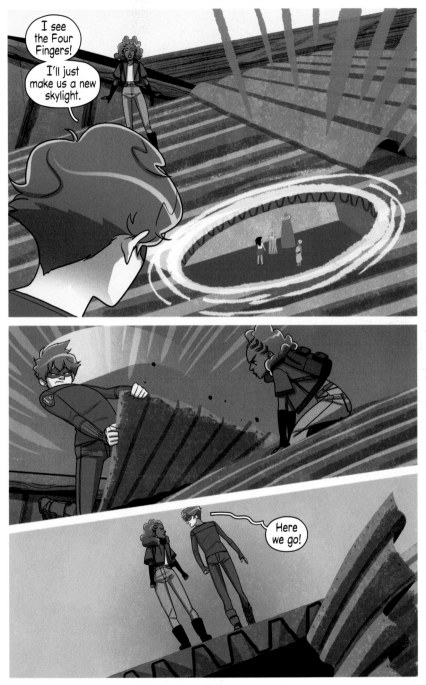

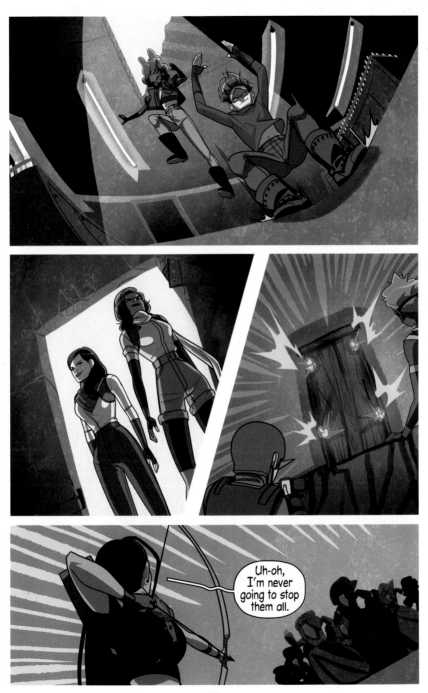

119

Psst!

Huh?

Oh, Jon, perfect! Let in the sunlight! Of course!

I will call the birds.

Spin, friends, spin. Cause the roof to let sunlight in.

125

Our spies tell me they are headed back toward the desert lab. Gather our warriors.

Fly! Fly, birds, fly. Take all machines out of the sky.

It's a lot to ask, but we need you all to help buy us time.

Your Highness, Empress-in-Waiting of Upper Landis, River Queen, Patron of all Feathered Things, and Guardian of Gree, I beg of you to permit us to serve you.

So granted.

Whoa. I guess sometimes you don't really know the person standing right next to you.

134

135

137

138

141

Excuse me, Governor General. Our space craft came under attack by a drone.

Did it? How unusual! Sorry to hear that.

You might want to investigate that before someone investigates you.

Please excuse me a moment.

Superman's back!

The space dust for the PolarShield Project!

The Earth is saved!

I have one half of the vaccine to cure Lois. The boys are after a sample of the virus.

That's wonderful news.

But we've lost track of them in Landis!

I can help find them, but I need you to keep a close eye on our governor general.

I think he's up to no good.

143

144

Footprints! She must be alive!

146

149

ridley pearson is an Edgar nominee, a Fulbright Fellow, and a #1 *New York Times* bestselling author of more than 50 award-winning suspense and young adult adventure novels. His novels have been published in two dozen languages and have been adapted for both network television and the Broadway stage. Ridley's middle grade series include *Kingdom Keepers, Steel Trapp,* and *Lock and Key.* His first original graphic novel, *Super Sons: The PolarShield Project* was published as the launch title for DC Graphic Novels for Kids. Ridley plays bass guitar in an all-author rock band with other bestselling writers (Dave Barry, Amy Tan, Mitch Albom, Scott Turow, Greg Iles, and occasionally Stephen King). He lives and writes in the Northern Rockies along with his wife, Marcelle.

Ile gonzalez illustrated her first comic strip while in kindergarten and she grew up to study fashion design in college. Deciding graphic storytelling was her first true love, she refocused her creative efforts and landed her first paid work at the digital storytelling company Madefire, working exclusively for them and co-creating their popular middle grade series *The Heroes Club*. Ile most recently illustrated *Super Sons: The PolarShield Project*, the launch title for the DC Graphic Novels for Kids imprint, and its sequel, *Super Sons: The Foxglove Mission*.

From the creator of the *Super Sons* series comes a thrilling adventure featuring an all-new group of heroes! Turn the page for a preview of *Indestructibles Book 1: The First Fracture* by *New York Times* bestselling author **Ridley Pearson** and artist **Berat Pekmezci**.

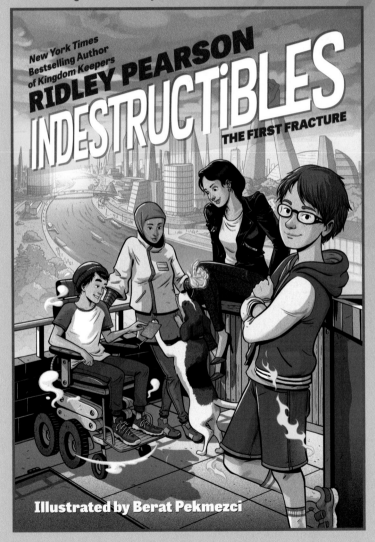

It's spreading quickly. Leave everything. We're getting out of here!

157

158

To be continued in **INDESTRUCTIBLES: THE FIRST FRACTURE!**